Commitment, the central them  certainly inspire and challenge the accomplishment.

Chaplain
Major General, Robert P. Taylor
USAF Retired Former Chief of Air Force Chaplains

Reaching Your Possibilities through Commitment is tremendously helpful. I could not avoid making new commitments and reaffirming some old ones as I read. Indeed, the book helped me become more happy and successful.

Dr. Ray Allen
Pastor, Blacksburg Baptist Church
Blacksburg, Virginia
Author of *How to Be a Christian*
Happy and Succcessful

The concept of commitment is a major theme in the Robert H. Schuller Institute for Successful Church Leadership. Gerald W. Marshall sheds new light on this age-old, but often overlooked, ingredient of success. His positive approach to commitment has grown out of the principles taught at the Institute and will help you grow in your commitments. Reading this book will motivate you to accept your role of leadership, set the goals, and pay the toll for success.

Wilbert B. Eichenberger

Reaching Your Possibilities

THROUGH COMMITMENT

Gerald W. Marshall

Other good Regal reading:
Courage to Love by Dan Montgomery
Strategy for Living by Edward R. Dayton
and Ted W. Engstrom
Lord, Make My Life a Miracle
by Raymond C. Ortlund

The foreign language publishing of all Regal
books is under the direction of GLINT.
GLINT provides financial and technical
help for the adaptation, translation and
publishing of books in more than 85 lan-
guages for millions of people worldwide.

For more information write: GLINT, P.O.
Box 6688, Ventura, California 93006.

Published by Regal Books
A Division of G/L Publications
Ventura, California 93006
Printed in U.S.A.

Library of Congress Catalog Card
No. 80-53140
ISBN 0-8307-0777-8

Dedication

To the Robert H. Schuller Institute for Successful Church Leadership and the Garden Grove Community Church, Garden Grove, California, for without their ministry this book would never even have been in the dreaming stage.

Contents

Foreword

A major source of personal energy, excitement, and enthusiasm is commitment. When you make a commitment, enormous power flows into your mind—brilliant flashes of insight explode within you! It is amazing what you are able to do, because you make a commitment.

Commitment is at the top of my list of seven life-changing human values. Commitment is where living really begins. This book is right on target in focusing on how to make and carry out commitments in life.

The principles set forth here by Gerald Marshall have grown out of the concepts I have taught and practiced in my ministry at Garden Grove Community Church and the "Hour of Power" telecast for many years. You can gain great self-confidence and power in your Christian life by applying these principles in your adventure of possibility thinking. Take them, use them, and live your possibilities!

Robert Schuller

Preface

Dr. Robert H. Schuller recently stated in an "Hour of Power" telecast, "Commitment is not corny, it is converting." And converting it is! Commitment can change your life. It can make you a whole new person and change your direction in life from a dull routine of daily existence to the exciting abundance of possibility living. You can reach your possibilities through commitment.

In this book I want to show you in very simple and easy-to-follow steps how you can revolutionize your life through making and carrying out specific commitments. In 1976 I discovered that each one of us has what I have called a *threshold of commitment.* This threshold of commitment is the level where you presently find yourself in your ability to make and carry out specific commitments in life. If you have a high threshold of commitment, it means you are highly committed to specific goals and are very successful in your ventures in life. If your threshold is low, it indicates that you do not make commitments or are unable to carry out specific commitments in your life.

During our adventure together in these pages, I want to share with you the *process of commitment*. You will learn that by practicing regularly the steps of this process, you can raise your threshold of commitment and become more successful. It is a simple process, but it is in no way "corny" because it can change your seemingly already successful life to a super success. You can multiply your abilities many times again and accomplish things that right now you feel are impossible for you. You can become a more productive Christian, a better parent, a better business or professional person. You will become more energetic, more enthusiastic, and more joyful in all that you do. As you raise your threshold of commitment you will gain more self-confidence, more spirituality, more personal power, and more direction in life. You will become a better person and your friends and associates will know it and be glad—and so will you.

This handbook is small, simple, and easy to read. It can become your regular companion and a workbook to blaze a path to your new life of possibility living through commitment. So fasten your seat belt and get ready for a trip from your aspirations to your attainments. Get ready to start doing, having, and becoming the things you once dared only to dream about. There is a way and you are on your way!

I would like to thank the many persons who helped make this book possible. First, thanks to Dr. Robert Schuller and the Robert H. Schuller Institute for Successful Church Leadership as well as the Garden Grove Community Church for inspiring me to raise my own threshold of commitment high enough to develop these concepts and put them in writing.

Then thanks to the many churches and chapels and ministers and lay friends who have allowed me to bounce these ideas off them and use their responses to prove the practicality of the threshold of commitment and the process of commitment.

Thanks also to those who have "field-tested" these concepts and proven that they are life-changing in the work-a-day world.

Thanks also to Mrs. Ruth Hughes for her many hours of typing assistance and to my wife, Sara, for her patient editorial help.

Thanks to everyone who had a part in helping make this dream a reality.

Have a good trip!

Gerald W. Marshall

Gerald W. Marshall

1
Your Inherent Potential

*You are to be perfect, as
your heavenly Father is perfect.*
Matthew 5:48

Your life is probably very much like an iceberg. The part that shows is a very small part of what is really there. The vast majority of your ability and potential is probably hidden below the surface and you may or may not even be aware that it is there. For instance, it is a known fact that we use less than 10 percent of our brain power. Over 90 percent is below the surface. The same principle is true of nearly every area of our lives.

How would you like to develop more of your hidden potential? To become more productive in life? More successful? Experience more of this fleeting thing called life in the same number of hours and days?

Hear ye, hear ye! Good news! You can get more out of life by raising your *threshold of commitment* through practicing the process of commitment.

It just so happens that within you is what we might call your "Inherent Potential." This is the peak level of performance you have designed into you if your full capabilities are developed in every area of life. In other words, God created you with certain abilities, talents, skills, and possibilities unique to you. While many of these elements are not fully developed or realized in your life, they are still there, below the surface, and they can be developed through specific commitments.

Let me illustrate from sports. You well know that in field and track competition today many mile runners are able to break the four-minute mile. But that was not done until after May 6, 1954 when Roger Bannister broke the four-minute barrier the first time on the Iffley Road Track in London. It was done through a combination of belief in the possibility, having the inherent ability, and total commitment to the task.

If Roger Bannister and his two pacers, Chris Chataway and Chris Brasher, had not specifically committed themselves to the breaking of the four-minute mile on that windy day, he would not have reached such a monumental accomplishment. In other words, his inherent potential was that of a sub-four-minute miler but he would never have developed that hidden potential without unwavering commitment to his goal.

After Roger broke the barrier, other runners began to believe they could do it also and today it is a common occurrence. In fact, his record was broken only one month later. John Landy broke Bannister's record, then Bannister broke Landy's record two months later with a 3:58.8 mile. At this writing, Sebastian Coe holds the record at 3:48.95. When Coe set the new mile record on July 17, 1979, at the Dubai Golden Mile race in Oslo, the first 10 finishers were all under four minutes. This confirms Bannister's early belief that the four-minute mile barrier was psychological, not physical.

Now the amazing thing is that the potential was there in Bannister all the time, below the surface. This makes me wonder how many runners before Bannister had the inherent potential but didn't believe they had and therefore didn't commit themselves to breaking the barrier.

Something else also makes me wonder: What is your inherent potential in any and every facet of daily life? Henry Ford once said, "There isn't a person anywhere who isn't capable of doing more than he thinks he can." Thomas Edison stated, "If we did all we are capable of doing, we would literally astonish ourselves."

Your inherent potential is so great that you are going to have a hard time believing how much power and ability you actually can develop. You see, God designed and created you just a little lower than the angels (see Ps. 8:5). You are the crown of His creation. He created you with abilities and powers and talents that you likely have not even dreamed of as yet. He made us with an eye to perfection. Oh, I know we will never be perfect, but the possibility is just beyond our fingertips if we are committed to Him and have His spirit working through us. Elton Trueblood says we are "called to greatness" and "to be small in any realm in which you can be large is obviously a sin against Almighty God."

To put it in very contemporary and practical terms, there is a bit of Superman in each of us. There is a superperson, a superself, lurking within, struggling to burst forth. It's that unrealized potential waiting and wanting to be developed; but it is being held down by a low threshold of commitment. The superself is shackled because we don't make firm and specific commitments to develop our inherent potential. We don't have enough faith in ourselves and our Creator to launch out into the deep of life, but rather we gently paddle along the shoreline, content with the daily routines of existence.

Each of us has a threshold of commitment. This is our present level of ability to make and carry out specific commitments in our daily routines of life. In reality, life and its living is a series of commitments. There are spiritual commitments, marriage and family commitments, business or professional commitments, and many personal commitments, such as health, recreation, education, and on and on. If we have a low threshold of commitment, it means we do not make and complete commitments as we should, often failing or—even worse—never trying. If the threshold is high, it means the person is successful in making and fulfilling specific commitments in life and is normally very active, productive, and confident.

A common and easy-to-understand example of the threshold is seen in dieting. Some individuals have started on dozens of different diets but somehow don't ever stay with one and still need to lose weight. They read about the latest high-fiber diet, for instance, and enthusiastically give it a try. But two weeks later they are searching for a better diet and the weight is still there. This is a typical low threshold of commitment. But the person who finds a diet plan, makes a firm and specific commitment to the program, sets targets or goals to lose a certain number of pounds in a given length of time, then sticks with the diet until the pounds are gone and the wardrobe is refitted, has a high threshold of commitment. We don't even have to ask which of these two people is happier about himself and is getting the most out of life.

Or, how about the Christian who wants to have a personal daily Bible reading and prayer time. He or she finally gets around to a quiet time with God, but two weeks later realizes it has just gradually fallen by the wayside. He or she makes another effort, and another, but to no avail. Diagnosis: a low threshold of commitment. Contrast that to the person who makes a firm and specific commitment to spend 15 minutes per day, first thing in the morning, in Bible reading. By using a good devotional guide and giving the time a certain priority, three months later that person is enjoying morning devotions and prayer more than the first day. Wow, that's great! A high threshold of commitment and going higher every day.

A person who develops a high threshold of commitment, and is enthusiastically accomplishing great things as a Christian, is sharing in the fullness of life which Jesus Christ came to earth to give us. He said in John 10:10, "I came that they might have life, and might have it abundantly." No one has made a greater impact on the world than Jesus Christ did in just three years of public activity. He showed us the abundance of life by living every moment to its fullest, doing great things for others. By His death on the cross He provided forgiveness of sin and by His resurrection assured us of eternal abundant life. Needless to say, Christ had a high threshold of commitment and developed His full inherent potential. A Christian is a son of God and a follower of Jesus Christ; therefore, we should follow Christ's example. We should fully commit our lives to God in Christ and develop our full potential in His Spirit. This is exactly what the apostles and disciples in the New Testament did and they turned the world upside down.

One of the beautiful things about developing a high threshold of commitment and realizing our potential is that we develop a good self-image and consequently good relationships with God and our fellowman. We realize what a fabulous creation God made us and how much He designed into us. We experience how wonderful it is to be alive and living abundantly. That makes us feel good about ourselves, good about God, others and His total creation. We develop a zest for living for God and others, a burning desire to serve and actively do His will. We hunger and thirst for righteousness because we realize that God has tucked deep within us a part of Himself that is living through us. In short, we realize that God engineered into us the ability to live life in all its splendor as we relate to Him and our fellowman.

You know what makes a good sports car perform like a

thoroughbred? Not a flashy red paint job and decals, or racing stripes on the outside. Not shiny exhaust pipes or flashy uphol- stery or chrome motor parts. The secret to a great sports car is the engineering designed into it by its designer. Our personal engineer is the very best. He is the master designer. Every human being is individually designed and engineered for opti- mum performance. Each a classic. Every one a Grand Prix winner!

Once we realize this greatness and potential that God has given to us and are committed to Him and to the development of our potential, nothing can hold us back. But contrast this image to one of a person who has a low threshold of commit- ment and accomplishes very little and consequently has a poor self-image. Fear of failure and a lack of self-confidence have caused a withdrawal from the cutting edge of abundant life. This person cannot adequately relate to his God and his fellowman because he cannot relate to himself. He or she may feel that providing for self and developing the self is wrong and sinful. He cannot be joyous without because he is not joyous within. Such a person needs first to study Christ's admonition to "love your neighbor as yourself" (Matt. 19:19) and realize that self- confidence or self-love is essential to loving your neighbor and living fullness of life. Christ is saying here that it is okay to care for yourself and develop your own self-worth. In fact, He is saying that your ability to love your neighbor is in proportion to your love of yourself. Once this is understood, you then can begin to gain self-confidence and develop your potential through making specific commitments and raising the threshold of commitment. Then you will begin to grow and share in the abundant life.

So, let's begin to explore your iceberg. Let's unveil your inherent potential, your superself. Just what is your potential in areas where you aspire to excel? Or do you have any aspira- tions?

2
Aspiring and Desiring

All things are possible to
him who believes.
Mark 9:23

What are your deepest, almost secret, aspirations and desires in life? Just how big would your dreams be if you were assured there was a way to bring your attainment up to your aspirations? Wow, such a thought can almost short-circuit your mind!

Napoleon Hill in his ever popular best-seller, *Think and Grow Rich*, uniquely reveals his secret of success that every attainment begins with an idea. Today man flies through the air at more than twice the speed of sound because he had the desire and idea to fly like the birds. Now no bird can fly like man in his sophisticated flying machines. Right now we can turn on a television in the comfort of our own home and instantly get a live picture, in vivid color and clear sound of an event half-way around the world while it is happening, all because of a series of big ideas that various individuals had about how to transmit sounds and pictures. It all had its beginning with the ideas of Marconi as he developed the first practical radio in 1895.

Many times when big-dreaming people had ideas of how to

do something that had never been done, they were scoffed at, laughed at, and even ostracized by their peers. But their dreams became reality. Where do you think our world would be today without the big dreams of persons like Leonardo da Vinci, Thomas Jefferson, Alexander Graham Bell, Ben Franklin, Henry Ford, Wernher von Braun, and other great thinkers through the ages? Where will we be in 25 years if we think small, or if we have a crop failure in the field of big aspirations and dreams?

It has often been said that we are only one generation from heathenism. Perhaps we are only one generation from the Dark Ages as well if we don't have big ideas. We need vivid imagination to create new ideas for success. Albert Einstein once said, "Imagination is everything. It is the preview of coming attractions." Napoleon said, "Imagination rules the world." If you will let your imagination dream up big ideas, you can rule your own life and make your preview of coming attractions become reality.

Considering your inherent potential and your imagination, what kind of dreams ought you to have in your hopper? If your superself were to begin to bloom, what kind of big ideas would you develop?

Many centuries ago there was a young lad named Joseph who was a dreamer. He dreamed two dreams where he visualized himself as ruler over his 11 brothers and his parents. This full and dramatic story is in the Old Testament in Genesis 37 through 45; but the conclusion of the saga is that Joseph eventually became second in command of all Egypt and truly did become a ruler over his family.

Joseph's dreams may well have been dreams that came to him at night while he was asleep, but they were in reality visions or aspirations of what he might potentially become in life. Who would ever have thought a young man who was sold into slavery, carried off to another country and thrown into jail could save a nation from famine and be ruler over millions? The inherent potential was there—and it blossomed! It became reality. God had designed into Joseph the potential of leadership, and Joseph's commitment to God and service to his fellowman made it possible for him to develop his inherent potential.

A young man named Dwight L. Moody was a shoe salesman when he came to the conviction that the world had yet to see a man fully committed to God. He conceived of the idea or dreamed the dream that he might be that first person wholly given to God. He committed himself to that goal and today you can read of his great ministry as a lay evangelist in the United States and England during the great revivals of the second half of the nineteenth century. He and his song leader, Ira Sankey, made one of the greatest impacts for Christ ever made by an evangelist of any age. Who would have believed a young shoe salesman, not even an ordained minister, could accomplish the task of winning thousands to Christ and enriching the Christian lives of hundreds of thousands?

You may be young or old, male or female, a shoe salesman, a keeper of sheep, a lawyer, teacher, or unemployed, but you have vast potential stored deep inside you like an underground fuel tank. And it will stay right there until the valve on the ground level rusts shut unless you dream big dreams and aspire to develop your life as God would have you do.

Oh, I know you are probably letting negative thoughts creep in. You might be asking yourself, Why should I want to do something big or have big dreams?

Why not? Why shouldn't you be the best person you possibly can be and do the most you can in your fourscore and seven years plus in this life?

Someone has said, "You see life as it is and ask why; I see life as it ought to be and ask, why not?" Let's look at it this way.

What would Egypt and the family of Jacob have done in the eighteenth century B.C. if Joseph had said, "I don't want to make any big splash. I'm content to be a slave." Or what would be the fate of the thousands who came to know Jesus Christ under the preaching of Dwight L. Moody if young Dwight had said, "I'll just be a shoe salesman. I don't dig these big dreams and commitment stuff."

Would you dare to dream and aspire to do something that has never been done before? To develop and perfect something that mankind needs that doesn't even exist today? I have a good friend who is an electrical technician and something of an inventor who dares to dream that he will one day invent an anti-gravity device. Sounds impossible? Well, so did telephones, television, airplanes, laser beams, and nearly everything else at one time. Watch the headlines and one day you may see that he accomplished it or a dozen other things almost as "impossible" in the process. Believeing is achieving! That concept is so true you had better be careful what you dream or you may find yourself doing it. Richard Bach, in his book *Illusions*, says, "You are never given a wish without also being given the power to make it true."

Some folks today have a wet blanket idea that everything has already been done or invented. In fact, I was talking to a young lady recently, who is a specialized instructor in her field, and she made the flat statement that there is nothing new left to be discovered in her specialty area. She said all there is left to do is teach what is already known. The truth is that there are no fields of endeavor or subjects that have been completely exhausted. Generation after generation has felt it has arrived at the apex of progress. The November, 1979, edition of *Bits and Pieces* told that in 1895 a commissioner of the U.S. Patent Office proposed to congress that the patent office be closed because all the great inventions had already been discovered.

That was before the days of automobiles, computers, space flight, and plastic, and the same year that Marconi perfected the radio. Most of the modern conveniences which we now take for granted were not even dreamed of then.

Every one of our wonders that surround us today began with an idea, an aspiration, a dream. We need to place an advertisement in every newspaper, "Wanted: Dreamers of the impossible today and the commonplace tomorrow. High risk but tremendous rewards. Begin today by turning on your imagination."

What kinds of dreams might you as a Christian have for your home, community, city, state, country or for the world at large? What challenges from God are still unmet today? Robert Schuller, in his Institute for Successful Church Leadership, says the secret of success is to "find a need and fill it, find a hurt and heal it." All we need do is look around us and we can see overwhelming need and hurt. Providing for and healing our fellowman is a task that nearest resembles perpetual motion—it never ends. Jesus commented that "the poor you always have with you" (Mark 14:7). How do you know but that within your brain lies a solution to world poverty? Or a cure for one of the many diseases that plague the world? Or a way to harness the weather—to prevent famine or too much rain or too violent cold?

Needs and hurts permeate our world like salt does the sea—they are everywhere. Spiritual, physical, psychological and social needs are present everywhere, in everyone, especially the affluent. World needs are so big it takes big dreams to find ways to alleviate them. The onrush of the masses today is so overwhelming that small dreams are like sticking your finger in the hole in the dike where a bulldozer went through!

Where do you fit into all this? You see, you are a uniquely created individual with that "iceberg" inherent potential, standing poised and ready to be launched like a missile at Cape Canaveral. You can be able to meet those pressing needs of our modern world, able to provide those creations not yet conceived, able to share in that abundant life that has not yet been lived—if you can start the process with big ideas, big aspirations and big dreams. Your superself is at the crucial point of breaking the seams if your aspirations will only set it free.

And that is where possibility living comes in.

3
Possibility Living

*Truly I say to you, if you
have faith as a mustard
seed, you shall say to
this mountain, "Move
from here to there," and
it shall move; and
nothing shall be
impossible to you.*
Matthew 17:20

Possibility living is the kind of living God created us to experience, that is, to become all that we can in the number of years we have on this earth. Not just to do what comes naturally, not just to exist, not just to live from hand to mouth till the clock runs down, but to live life to its fullest, to excel at the greatest of the fine arts—living!

Possibility living is big thinking, big believing, positive thinking, and possibility thinking all meshed together and put into practice in your work-a-day world. It is experiencing with zest the vibrations of existence in the presence of the Creator and His creation from Monday morning through Sunday evening.

Possibility living is waking in the morning, refreshed, with the feeling, "This is the day which the Lord has made; let us rejoice and be glad in it" (Ps. 118:24), and closing the day with, "Thank you, Lord, for the great experiences and relationships of this day." It is like living a life of all red-letter days, like living on the plus side of the ledger instead of the minus. It's an explosion of the sensation of being!

To use the new terminology you are learning, *possibility living* is the development of your inherent potential and letting the superself dawn within you. It is developing a high threshold of commitment and accomplishing your dreams in life. In short, it is living the abundant life, both physically and spiritually.

One of the key indicators of abundant life and possibility living is growth. I have a poster hanging in my office that says, "The only evidence of life is growth." Many of our lives are like some of the plants I've also had in my office, right along with the poster. They didn't grow. They just sat there until finally they faded and withered away, never bearing any blooms or fruit. The reason these plants did not grow is because they could not get enough sunlight. Several of them did not grow because they didn't get enough water—or was it too much water?

Just as a plant needs the proper balance of water, food and light, so our lives need the proper balance of big dreams, possibility thinking, and commitment to bear the fruit of the abundant life. Possibility living is living life in that balance as it was designed by God to be lived, in all its splendor and excellence.

Every coin has two sides. There is always the other side of the story and possibility living has its other side also. The opposite of possibility living is impossibility living. You have heard people say, "You can't do that," or "That is impossible." Impossibility living people are, as my father used to say when I was a boy, "moving so slow you have to sight them on a fence post to see if they are moving." If you can get a good sturdy fence post lined up just right, you will usually find that they are moving all right, but backward instead of forward. Life is a downhill run, but down the wrong side of the hill!

Impossibility living is too often the average life—possibility living is the exception. But it could and should be the other way around. Not enough people really believe in themselves and the abilities and powers available to them from the Creator. When Christ said if you just have the faith of the smallest mustard seed, nothing will be impossible to you, He wasn't putting out idle words. He wasn't giving us a teaching we are incapable of following. Often we try to find a way to explain away the meaning of those words. But Christ really meant what He said. Within our own lives, through faith, lives the Almighty God Himself in the form of His Holy Spirit. God created the heavens and the earth. He put the galaxies in their places and keeps them all in their orbits. He has made the blind to see, the lame to walk, the dead to rise. He is the source of all power and all life; so with God all things are possible. If God is at work in us in proportion to our faith, then He is limited only by our lack of faith.

I can assure you that the possibilities within your own inherent potential right now are so great compared to your present accomplishments that they qualify as your "impossible." Develop your inherent potential with God's help and the impossible will have been performed in your life.

The great Napoleon Hill has said time and again, "Whatever the mind of man can conceive and believe, it can achieve." That's possibility living. It is conceiving the possibilities of what we should and can become and achieve—being confident that God has given us a part of His own power, and achieving those possibilities.

Now comes the big $64,000 question that has been lurking behind all we have said thus far. How do you go about fulfilling your dreams and aspirations, developing your potential, and practicing possibility living? Read on my friend.

4
Commitment—The Master Key

*I press on toward the goal
for the prize of the upward
call of God in Christ Jesus.*
Philippians 3:14

Paul Meyer, president of Success Motivation International, writes, "No other force in the world—psychological or material—can equal the indomitable drive of a man who has committed himself to the achievement of a personal goal." Dr. Rollo May, outstanding psychologist, writer, and lecturer, states, "A man or woman becomes fully human only by his or her choices and his or her commitments to them." Dr. Denis Waitley says in his *Psychology of Winning,* "Achievement is almost automatic when the goal becomes an inner commitment."

Each of the three eminent authorities quoted above is addressing a different subject from a different perspective, but each of them refers to one common ingredient—commitment. Commitment is the bottom line of individual growth and development; it is the universal ingredient in accomplishment; commitment is the master key to success.

Success in any venture is multi-faceted to say the least. There are many "key" ingredients which play major roles in various techniques, systems, or approaches to personal success. Some of the keys to success are: goal setting, positive thinking, knowledge, big thinking, big believing, positive mental attitude, motivation, enthusiasm, persistence, and many more. But in reality, none of these elements alone or in combination will bring true and lasting success unless it is undergirded by commitment. There must be grass-roots commitment behind your goals, enthusiasm, motivation or positive thinking. The master key must be used in conjunction with the other keys.

About three miles from our home we have a safety deposit box in a local bank where we keep some of our most valuable and treasured family items. Recently I went there to add several documents to its contents. I took my key to the box with me but before I could open the box the young lady at the bank had to insert the master key into the stainless steel drawer door. Then I placed my key in its slot and the box effortlessly slid out, revealing its treasured contents.

Success is like the contents in the double-locked safety deposit box—you can't reach it without the master key. Neither enthusiasm, motivation, positive thinking, nor any of the other keys to success will work alone without basic commitment.

Let me illustrate. A young, positive-thinking graduate student was in desperate need of money to stay in school and provide for his family. He was searching for a way to make a good income and continue his studies at the same time. He was introduced to a new direct sales product which had a good commission and was a natural for him to sell. With great enthusiasm he made his initial investment, attended several sales meetings, and started showing the product to his selected prospects. He knew his product well and even believed in its worth to his customers. However, about six weeks later he had made no sales, was discouraged, and was looking for a more suitable job. He was a total failure because he had not committed himself to the task. He somehow thought the product would sell itself, or that his enthusiasm and motivation would carry him to success. He had expected some sort of magic to bring him money without ever really involving himself. After about four or five presentations and polite "no thanks," he lost his enthusiasm and decided sales was not his line of work.

If this young "would be" salesman had committed himself to the task he would have gained persistence and drive to add to his enthusiasm, motivation, and positive thinking. He then would not have quit before he had made enough presentations to merit a sale.

Now I know this story is true, because I was that potential salesman. I am certain commitment was the missing link because, after I discovered the basic steps of the process of commitment, I realized I had not followed a single one of the steps. I never really involved myself. I was on the sideline wanting something for nothing. With a firm and specific commitment and knowledge of what it takes to fulfill a commitment, I feel I could have been an outstanding success. But no master key, no treasures.

Well, just what is this element called commitment that can turn the tide from failure to success with a single generous application? To begin with, commitment seems to mean many different things to different people. We hear ministers, salesmen, and public speakers regularly talking about making commitments and being committed but we don't always know what it means. It appears that most people accept being committed as some kind of intangible, illusive, almost mystical ingredient in life that we either have or do not have. It is a hit or miss, uncontrollable state of being that is closely associated with present emotions. As long as the emotional state is high, the commitment is strong; but when depression or other negative emotions strike, commitment goes out the window. Commitment also seems to be related to physical feelings. When we are feeling well, commitment is strong; but when pain or discomfort enters the picture, commitment goes by the wayside. Commitment is something we all talk about but often don't know from whence it comes or whither it goes.

The word *commit* is a verb with the basic meaning of "to do or to perform." As we are using it here, it means "to bind or involve yourself or to pledge." *Commitment* is the noun form indicating the act or process of committing, or, in our context, "a binding pledge or a promise." Commitment in its highest form, the kind of commitment that converts and changes, is getting involved with action. It is a pledge being carried out to completion. It is putting your total self on the line. It is not idle words, not superficial pretense, not hollow promises, and not rote action. Commitment is inward and outward giving of the total you to a purpose, a cause, an activity, a person, an idea or ideal, an organization or an object. It is an engaging of the self in action, either physical, mental or spiritual, with purpose and direction. It is risky but rewarding, requires sacrifice but reaps sumptuously. Without commitment, life is play-acting with no involvement. With commitment, life is fulfilling.

When closely analyzed, commitment is actually a process which can be learned and practiced at will. It can be initiated by purposely making specific commitments. It also can be controlled to the point that one might grow in the ability to be committed and thus be more successful and productive in life. This procedure is called raising the threshold of commitment.

The threshold of commitment can be systematically raised by intentionally making small but challenging commitments at first, then making larger and larger commitments. When you complete a small commitment and enjoy the results, you gain confidence in your own ability and are ready to make larger commitments. Each time a commitment is completed, the threshold is elevated right along with self-esteem, personal abilities, and abundance of life. The more you succeed, the higher will be your threshold. It is through this process that you can realize your inherent potential and enjoy possibility living.

Persons who know the meaning of commitment and raise their threshold of commitment to a high level give commitment a very high priority. Bart Starr, famed coach of the Green Bay Packers says, "Commitment is the name of the game." Robert Schuller puts commitment as number one on his list of seven life-changing values. Dr. Robert E. Naylor, president emeritus of Southwestern Baptist Theological Seminary says, "Christian commitment makes the difference."

Commitment really made a difference in the lives of the apostles in the New Testament, especially the apostle Paul. He was perhaps the most committed follower of Jesus Christ of all time. He showed that he was constantly raising his threshold of commitment when he said in Philippians 3:14 "I press on toward the goal for the prize of the upward call of God in Christ Jesus." He then showed in 4:13 just how much confidence he had and how strong his commitment really was. He said, "I can do all things through Him who strengthens me." In spite of being in jail, beaten, stoned, shipwrecked and having a thorn in the flesh, he did more to spread Christianity and apply the teachings of Christ than any other person of any age. He was a man totally involved in faith in action. Ultimately he proved his total commitment by giving his life for the cause of Christ.

Dr. Robert Schuller is a modern example of commitment in action. His story of faith and commitment goes from the sticky tar-paper roof of the Orange Drive-in-Theater to the beauty and splendor of the Crystal Cathedral. His unwavering commitment has taken the Garden Grove Community Church from a group of people in 50 automobiles listening on drive-in-theater speakers to millions all over the world being blessed weekly by the

"Hour of Power" television ministry. Commitment is his way of life and possibility thinking has elevated his threshold of commitment to the top of the chart.

Those who have learned the process of commitment have overcome obstacles that loomed before them like mountain peaks with no visible passes between them. Their stories are miraculous—persons who were told they would never walk again becoming competitive marathon runners; businessmen who lost everything, sometimes several times, and today are millionaires; students who flunked out of college but now hold doctorates; internationally acclaimed public speakers who once stammered and stuttered and were afraid of crowds; and youth raised in log cabins, ghettos, and poverty holding the highest offices in the land. Commitment makes the difference.

But for the threshold of commitment to be raised, commitment must be understood as a process which can be learned. There are very distinguishable steps which one must go through to become committed or to make a commitment. If this process is followed, it is possible for individuals to attain what once seemed impossible for them. These steps of commitment are simply the basic process which successful individuals have been using throughout the ages to attain, perform, and become what they desire. Productive people have used this process regularly but may never have been aware of the steps nor written them out for others to emulate. Persons who have been unsuccessful in their lives either do not seem to be aware of this process or violate its steps, and are left bouncing back and forth between emotions and feelings, needs and wants, and never seem to get their act together. Some who are unsuccessful know the process but choose not to follow it, because they are not willing to pay the price to succeed. They often lack discipline or motivation because they are entirely too comfortable in their failures and the status quo.

The person with the history of failures has a low threshold of commitment and is unable to raise the threshold because he or she does not practice the process of commitment. The successful and productive individual has somehow learned and practiced the process of commitment and thus has raised the threshold to a high level.

I believe God wants each one of us to develop a high threshold of commitment. He wants us to be committed—to be successful in the life He has given to us. God didn't create us to be failures. He didn't create the beauty of life and give us all our fabulous faculties for us to be a flop. What a waste! As we have often heard, "God don't make no junk." God is not a junk dealer. He is a connoisseur of fine beings and fine living. To be living in the mire of mediocrity is like a racehorse pulling a plow, a Rolls Royce in a demolition derby, or Roger Staubach playing "Simon Says."

We were created for success, and commitment is the master key to success, so let's begin opening up some of those double-locked doors and get to the treasures of accomplishment. Let us look briefly at the steps of commitment and learn how to apply them to our own daily lives.

Actually there are four basic steps in the process of commitment, or the 4 C's of commitment. The four steps all start with the letter *C* so that you can more easily remember them and apply them in your life. The 4 C's are (1) *choosing* your commitment, (2) *committing* yourself firmly and specifically, (3) *coordinating* all your resources toward fulfilling your commitment, and (4) *completing* your commitment. Under each step there are several sub-steps which we will cover in detail later as we move along. These basic steps are the things you must do in some way to be totally successful in any venture in life.

Take a very common example that is the basic unit of our society—marriage. A good marriage follows these four steps precisely. It all begins with that natural and enjoyable process which young people engage in, sometimes for years, courtship. The ultimate goal of the courtship process is to find the young man or young lady you want to commit yourself to in marriage. This is step 1, choosing your commitment. Marriage is a commitment of the highest degree and one of the most important commitments most people make. It should be a lifetime commitment. As my Christian ethics professor, Dr. T.B. Maston, said time and again, it is "one man, one wife, for life."

Once the young couple falls in love and decides they are the right ones for each other, then comes step 2, making the firm and specific commitment—the marriage ceremony. Whether in the church or by a justice of the peace or a ships's captain, it goes something like this. "Do you John take Jane to be your wedded wife . . . for better or for worse . . . till death shall part you?" My friend, the commitment becomes firm and specific when they sign their names on the dotted line of the license. Normally to whatever degree the couple takes the marriage as a total commitment, so is the degree of success in the relationship.

After choosing and committing, the marriage then needs step 3, coordination of all the available resources to make the relationship beautiful and harmonious. Even the very best marriages need to utilize the help provided by the teachings of the church and Scripture, parents who set a good example, books that inspire them, banks who lend them money, and a thousand other sources of assistance. In the problem marriage there are marriage counselors, ministers, doctors, and a host of people who can help them make the marriage better so that the commitment can be fulfilled. All the couple has to do is ask for and accept the help available to them.

Step 4 is one that goes on for the rest of life as you complete the commitment. Stay with the commitment "till death shall part you" and you will bear all kinds of fruit of marriage: children, grandchildren, a beautiful life together, silver wedding anniversary, growing closer as the years go by. A marriage with no commitment usually lasts only a short time and often ends in heartache, bitterness, alimony, estranged children, and a world of frustration. Good marriages follow the four steps to the letter. Bad marriages violate steps along the way. I personally have performed over 270 weddings and have followed through in counseling with many of the couples. I have also counseled with hundreds of other married couples with problems and, almost without exception, a short courtship—poor choosing phase, step 1—makes for a rocky or failing marriage. Those who take the marriage ceremony only as a legal requirement and do not make a firm commitment are committing marital suicide. Couples who do not seek help or refuse help from available sources when problems arise, usually don't last long enough to bear the fruit of a good family. Out there in the jungle of the daily world many couples are struggling in their marriages because of lack of commitment.

Let us look for a moment at the Christian commitment of faith that results in salvation. This too must follow the four basic steps. First comes the choosing phase, step 1: Do I want to be a Christian? Do I want to follow Jesus Christ and repent of my sins? When the decision is made in a Sunday School class, a revival meeting, a church service, or in your home, next comes the firm and specific commitment to Jesus Christ, step 2, as revealed in the Scriptures. This may be before a church in a public profession, to a counselor at a crusade, to a friend, a parent, or perhaps in your own solitude. But somewhere, sometime, a commitment must be made. The commitment must be self-giving to a Person, Jesus Christ. This is called being born again, accepting Christ as Saviour, taking your stand for God, or a host of other things in different groups. Next comes a pastor's class, Bible study programs, worship, fellowship, prayer meetings, church organizations—step 3, coordinating your resources and those of others and of God to carry out your commitment. Finally, the commitment is only valid and worthwhile if you stay with it, step 4, until the fruits of abundant life and eternal life are reaped, until it is completed.

This same process is essential for total success in smaller day-by-day or even one-time immediate commitments. Take getting a college degree. Step 1 is deciding whether you even want to get an education or not, choosing the school, and deciding on a major. You may commit yourself to getting a degree years before you begin, but applying for entrance and registration, step 2, makes it firm and specific and gives you some goals to shoot for. Step 3 is coordinating help toward that degree by learning from professors, fellow students, the library, and getting financial aid from parents or a job or a student loan. Step 4 is the clincher, staying with the commitment until it is completed. Only after you take the full curriculum can you put on the cap and gown and receive the degree from the dean.

Thousands of parents spend money every year on students who violate the steps. They go to college because parents choose it for them. They don't study because they didn't make the commitment or because they don't want to discipline themselves to the task. Many drop out after two semesters or two years and consequently never see the sheepskin. That is a low threshold of commitment or no commitment at all. Such major failures in a young adult may cause him or her never to realize more than five percent of his or her inherent potential. The iceberg may even sink.

These same steps in the process of commitment apply to every area of endeavor: as a Christian evangelist, a teacher, a mother or father, to a diet, an exercise program, business ventures, vocations, professions, and even to hobbies, recreation, and entertainment. Life after all is a series of commitments, and success in life is fulfilling your commitments. If there are no commitments, life is meaningless. There is no involvement, and no fruit.

So, let's press on and explore in detail the 4 C's of commitment and learn how to apply them in our quest for possibility living and abundant life.

5

Step 1—Choosing Your Commitment Wisely

*Choose for yourselves
today whom you will serve.
Joshua 24:15*

Choosing—freedom of choice—perhaps the most awesome responsibility man has on earth. The ability to make conscious decisions, to accept or reject, to evaluate and conclude, to make moral and spiritual decisions, makes man closer to the image of God than any other living creation. It is man's unique power and his claim to fame, but can be the beginning of his end as well.

God gave man this dangerous ability at creation so that he would be free: free to accept or reject; free to be or not to be; free to turn to God or turn away from Him. God created man and woman with no strings attached.

This freedom is so commonplace to us and so seemingly easy that we take it for granted most of the time. We seldom realize what potential for better or for worse we face at a point of choice. Sometimes a single choice can change the course of our entire life or the lives of our families, or the community, yea, even the course of the world itself. Freedom of choice is not to be taken lightly but as a divine privilege and responsibility.

Success or failure in every aspect of life is a conscious decision. By our decisions we choose to fail or succeed. By our lack of conscious decision to succeed, we fail by default. As Harvey Cox says in a poster, "Not to decide is to decide." Sometimes we forfeit the game of life by our own lack of positive choice to make commitments and succeed.

Success actually begins with a conscious, rational decision to put wings to an idea, an aspiration, or a dream. A decision is a beginning and beginning is half done, so to choose wisely is half the battle.

But many people do not even go through a process to make a choice in commitments. Too often commitments are spur of the moment reactions. Of course, when a choice is made rapidly, without proper thought or no thought at all, the results are usually proportionate—shallow, short-lived, and meaningless. Or they may even result in turmoil and destruction. If a commitment is made that should not have been entered into and failure results, it can be destructive to the personality of the individual.

In the Old Testament, Joshua, the great leader of the children of Israel after Moses died, called the people to a decision: "Choose for yourselves today whom you will serve" (see Josh. 24:15). He was calling them to go through a process of thought that would result in a decision of commitment to either the God of their fathers or the gods of the Amorites. Elijah called the Israelites to the same type of decision between God and Baal many years later. Before we can make a commitment we must go through a process of choosing. The process must be thorough and accurate or the results will be harmful.

This principle of choosing is true in many areas of our daily lives. We have already mentioned that a quick or wrong decision in marriage can result in multiple problems. Sometimes young adults decide suddenly to join the military service. In basic training they realize they made a major commitment without a proper process of choosing; so they decide they want a discharge. Then there is the nice young couple who buys a full set of encyclopedias, dictionary, and annual volumes from a salesman at the door and, before the first child even comes along, is searching for someone to take over their monthly payments. Or how many Sunday School teachers say yes in the church vestibule when asked to teach a class, then drop out a month later because they didn't take the time to make a wise decision before committing themselves.

So, the first step in the time-proven process of commitment is to involve yourself in *wisely choosing whether you should or should not make a certain commitment.*

Can you imagine trying to carry out a commitment that you didn't have the privilege of choosing personally? How would you like to marry someone chosen for you by a friend? Or how would you like to accept a job chosen for you by a stranger. This happens from time to time but is usually a burden or a total failure. For instance, how many ministers have dropped out of the ministry or priesthood because they went to school and were ordained as a result of their parents deciding for them that the clergy was their calling in life? What is essential for success is for you to make your own decisions and make them wisely. You should not be committed to doing things that you do not want to do.

In something of a parenthesis, let me say that what you are attempting to do here in raising your threshold of commitment by making specific commitments is not to lay a heavy burden upon yourself. I am not trying to talk you into doing things that you don't want to do just to be successful. Quite the contrary. Commitments you make should be your own free choice. They should be things you want to do because they will bring more abundance to your life. You should make commitments that will help you to grow and develop your possibilities and to gain more self-confidence and power in life. Your commitments should be enjoyable and bring you happiness. God is not trying to coerce you into doing things you don't want to do either. If you commit your life to God, He will inspire you to want to do the things that are His will for you. But you make the decision to do what you want. Possibility living is your conscious choice.

Determining what you should commit yourself to is a process in itself. There are several sub-steps which will make it easier and more accurate as you choose. First you need to gather some information.

A. Be certain you have the facts.

You should become your own private investigator. You need to know everything possible about the what, why, when, where, and how of this activity or thing you are considering as a commitment. Not to know the facts prior to making a decision and launching out is to flirt with failure. This happened in my early adventures in running many years ago.

I decided several times that I needed more exercise, so I decided very superficially that I would start jogging. But I didn't get any facts or investigate the subject. I did everything wrong. I put on my old heavy sneakers, worn out at that, and went out in the heat of the day in Arizona to start my jogging program. Twice I started and lasted only about one block! My threshold of commitment and my self-confidence went down as a result of those experiences.

Then in October, 1968, I purchased Dr. Kenneth Cooper's brand new book on aerobics and read it thoroughly from cover to cover. There were the plain facts about running, and I said to myself, "I've got to have a piece of that action." I followed Dr. Cooper's instructions, which were derived from accurate research, and I have been running regularly ever since.

Read books, talk to people, perhaps do some research

yourself, but get the latest word on that which you are considering as a commitment. If it's marriage, find out about his or her family, learn of childhood days, find out how your prospective spouse reacts under stress, what are his or her money habits and attitudes, and on and on. Finding out important facts that you don't like after the honeymoon may be too late. Look before you leap!

Don't commit yourself to 36 months of payments on a "new" used car owned by the "little old school teacher from Pasadena who only drives on Sunday" and then find out it was owned by the local teenage drag king. A few free facts may be worth a fortune.

B. Imagine possibilities if you do or do not commit yourself.

Imagination is worth more than half the kingdom. A little "image-ing," as Norman Vincent Peale often calls it, can go a long way toward a right decision. Practicing possibility thinking, as advocated by Dr. Robert Schuller, may bring a lot of success or save you from a lot of failure in the years to come. We need desperately to be able to let our imaginations run freely and visualize all the possible good and bad which could lurk within a pending decision. Perhaps a period of daydreaming of all the wonderful things which could come from this commitment needs to be weighed alongside a time of "day-nightmaring" to imagine what your future could be like if you do not make the commitment.

For this step to work effectively, we need to develop optimistic, possibility imagination. We don't need to cultivate a pessimistic imagination as it is usually already overactive in most of us. We need to be able to capture in our minds the possibilities in an idea. We need to be like two young boys in a story I read when I was a young boy myself. These two aspiring businessmen of about 10 years of age found the skeleton of a cow in a pasture one day while playing. They were excited about their discovery and began to imagine how they could profit from their find.

Suddenly one of the boys realized that the handles on his new pocket knife were made of bone. They reckoned that the bone handles were worth at least one-quarter of the price of the knife and that they could sell the raw bones at perhaps half that price. So they began to measure how many handles could be made from the various bones and they began to get excited. With some simple calculations they had learned in arithmetic classes they imagined themselves with more money than they had ever dreamed of having before.

Naturally, when they got the skeleton to the market they learned a few facts about laws of supply and demand and the high cost of processing, manufacturing, and distribution and their bubble was burst. But, wow, what imaginations! That kind of boyhood imagination tempered with a few facts about the business world has made many persons wealthy. It can help you in choosing your commitment as well.

When I considered my decision to become a runner for fun and fitness, I imagined what great physical, mental, and spiritual strength and energy I could have at 50, 60, 70 and even 100 years of age if I kept my body in top physical condition through aerobic exercises. I also imagined how I could deteriorate and get run-down at those same ages if I continued with my old sedentary way of life. I seasoned those thoughts with some of my experiences as a chaplain ministering to persons of my own age and younger who had suffered through heart attacks where overweight and inactivity were probably contributing factors, and I decided I wanted to avoid that trip as long as possible. My thought process was closely parallel to the words of a clever little song that the queen of country music, Loretta Lynn, used to sing that says, "Everybody wants to go to heaven, but nobody wants to die."

After getting the facts and using positive and negative imagination, it was easy to make a lifetime commitment to running for fun and fitness. I have been running regularly now for well over a decade and I am enjoying it more than my hyperactive imagination ever dreamed I could.

C. Ask, will this be a great thing for myself, others and God's Kingdom?

Cavett Roberts, of Humaneering Incorporated of Memphis, Tennessee, says the way to solve problems is to "ask questions, ask questions." So it is time to ask yourself some searching questions to help decide if you should make that commitment.

The first thing you ask is, will this be good for me? Of course, some folks feel that we shouldn't do things for ourselves, only for others and Christ. Naturally serving Christ through others should be our greatest desire, but I can't conceive of anything that would be good for others and the Kingdom of God that would not also profit us, and that is good. If we don't derive some benefits from serving, it is not likely that we would continue the service.

So it is okay to commit ourselves to things that we profit from. In fact, that should be one of our primary motives. When we commit ourselves to activities that make us a better person, we will be making it possible to better meet others' needs and will bring glory to the Kingdom of God. For example, we should commit ourselves to further our education since the knowledge we gain enables us to become better teachers and leaders. We should commit ourselves to getting more exercise and eating better food, for in so doing we are caring for the temple of the Holy Spirit and will reap more energy to meet human needs as well as be a better witness. We should commit ourselves to personal Bible study, for then we can rightly divide the Word of God and be a greater influence on others.

If when you ask this question, your answer is, "No, there is nothing great about this commitment for me, others or the Kingdom of God," you should proceed cautiously to the next step. If you find that there is something harmful about the commitment, you will probably throw out the commitment at this point and consider another commitment.

If this big dream or positive idea that you are considering as a commitment results in the answer "Yes, it will be a great thing for me, others, and God's Kingdom," you will very likely want to make the commitment and carry it out, because it is "great" things you are looking for, great things that will develop your potential and help you experience possibility living. Before you make your final decision though, give consideration to two more thoughts.

D. Ask, what are the moral, ethical or spiritual obligations?

There are still some "oughts" and "ought nots" in life in spite of some opinions. Your objective is to find out what your own "oughts" and "ought nots" are in life. My suspicion is that we should be more concerned about what we ought to do in our lives than what we ought not to do. Scholars tells us that the Golden Rule as proclaimed by Jesus Christ was around long before He proclaimed it. But it was stated negatively. It taught not to do to others as you would have others not do to you. But Christ made it positive. He put action to it. He told us to do to others as we would have others do to us. That is the kind of direction we should put on our living.

So what ought you to do in this commitment? Do you have a moral, ethical or spiritual obligation to do this thing under consideration? I feel certain that we should put wings on a lot more ideas than we do. For instance, we ought to take better care of our bodies. Jimmy Durante once said, "If I'd known I was going to live this long, I woulda taken better care of myself."

Romans 12:1 says: "Present your bodies a living and holy sacrifice, acceptable to God, which is your spiritual service of worship." That is just one of the spiritual obligations we have as a part of the abundant life. This obligation includes proper diet, proper exercise, proper rest, and proper activity with our bodies. That is a big "ought" but it is one which could do a lot for you, others, and God's Kingdom. It holds within it some wonderful possibilities to help you develop your inherent potential and find more success in life. When we start talking about spiritual obligations in the Scripture, we could easily use that as a basis to decide what commitments should be considered in our choosing process. Keep in mind that the more positive commitments you make and fulfill the higher your threshold of commitment will be and the more meaningful your life.

If you do discover that the commitment you are considering is spiritually, morally or ethically wrong, stop the train! Possibility living does not include wrongdoing; it is constructive, positive, upbuilding, and within laws of the land and laws of conscience and the Spirit. Those realms certainly include enough grounds that you have no need to go outside them. Staying within this concept is not restrictive at all. In fact, when seen positively, they open up your life to true freedom and assure that there will be no fetters as side effects. Any transgression of a law in order to gain freedom of action has an opposite reaction that is binding and takes away freedom.

Often the loss of freedom or restriction is only a risk, but the consequences are too high to flirt with. For instance, to commit yourself to be somewhere at a certain time that requires you to drive faster than the speed limit is to risk being caught speeding and being fined or jailed—or worse, wrecking and destroying life or property. This restriction or destruction far outweighs the small amount of time saved and you ultimately risk not being able to complete the commitment at all. Law-breaking is not a part of possibility living, so keep your commitments within moral, ethical, and spiritual obligations.

E.   Seek guidance through Scripture and prayer.

If any of these sub-steps could stand alone in the process of choosing, this one comes the closest. If there is still doubt after the first four considerations, this should give the answer clearly. Perhaps this should be the first consideration!

The Scripture is not a list of dos and don'ts nor does it have a direct answer for every situation. But it does contain the principles and guidelines for every situation if you study it, live it, and seek its wisdom. There are many people who study the Scripture and come up with different answers to the same problem. Therein lies one of the unique wonders of God's living Word. Each individual must find his or her own answers for his or her own specific problems and challenges. God works in many mysterious and wonderful ways with different people at different times. But He does work through His Word and the answers are there, and we can find them.

Prayer linked with Scripture is a powerful guidance system. One of the miracles of our age is computer guidance systems used to guide and direct missiles into space. But when you consider that they are nothing but human-programmed systems linked to the minds of men, you realize the power of prayer in that it is the mind of God linked with the mind of man. Prayer is personal two-way communication between you and the infinite almighty God. "Ask, and it shall be given to you; seek, and you shall find; knock, and it shall be opened to you" (Matt. 7:7). You ask and God will answer if you are spiritually attuned to His communications through the whole experience of life. That is a powerful guidance system. Prayer is powerful stuff. A little bit goes a long way, but a lot goes even further. Apply generously for guaranteed results.

Now that all the criteria for decision-making has been fed into the computer of your being, a decision is made concerning your proposed commitment. If the answer is no, you either modify the commitment or start over with a new idea. If the answer is yes, you then go on to step 2 in the process of commitment, knowing that this commitment is worthy of your very best effort because you have chosen it through a rational process. You are now on your way to success!

6
Step 2—Commit Yourself Firmly and Specifically

*As for me and my
house, we will serve the Lord.*
Joshua 24:15

After Joshua challenged the people of Israel to make a choice, he made his own choice and made his public commitment to "serve the Lord." Today we have it written in the book of Joshua for all to see for all times. From the information that follows in the book of Joshua we see that he lived up to that commitment till death.

In step 1 we talked about making your choice. Now that you have completed the choosing phase of the process of commitment, move on to step 2 and *make a firm and specific commitment.* As you choose and make the commitment you answer the "what" of the commitment. We will deal with the "when, where, and how much" under setting targets in sub-step B. When you actually make the commitment you will want to write it out on a "Steps of Commitment Worksheet" included in the back of the book in chapter 12. We will also talk more specifically in chapter 9 about the wording and value of writing out the commitment.

I use two very definite words here in relation to your commitment, "firmly" and "specifically." By firmly we mean serious and binding. Now I don't mean the kind of serious that makes life a drudgery but the kind that makes life meaningful, productive, and enjoyable. Most people don't seem to be very serious about their commitments, because they keep breaking them. When a commitment is made after a clear process of deciding, as was done in step 1, it should be binding—that is, if you are serious about developing your potential and being successful.

In the Old Testament when a Hebrew made a vow to God, it was serious business. Ecclesiastes 5:4,5 says you should fulfill a vow as soon as possible. To a Hebrew his word was binding. That seems to be one of the biblical concepts that has fallen through the cracks in being passed from Old Testament times through New Testament times and on to our modern age. Commitments are basically the same as Old Testament vows and should be fulfilled. Ecclesiastes also says it is worse to make a vow and not keep it than not to make one at all. We should say what we mean and mean what we say and take our commitments seriously.

I know many people advocate that we should not take ourselves or life too seriously. I agree that we should not get so serious about living and getting ahead that we get ulcers. But neither should we relax to the point that life runs through our fingers without our getting the very most out of every precious moment. Those moments add up to hours and hours add up to days, and they go by all too quickly if they are not properly utilized.

When we are young, we seem to think time is in unlimited supply. But, as we mature, we suddenly realize that our days are numbered and should be accepted as pearls of great price. If you don't think time and life are serious, go down to your local neighborhood funeral parlor some day and see how serious it seems when it is all gone.

In addition to firmly you should commit yourself "specifically." All too often our commitments, if we make them at all, are too general: "I'm going to live a better life." "I'm going to get in better shape." "I want to be a better Christian." That is like saying, "Head for the roundhouse, they will never corner you there." How can you miss? That is like a sawed off shotgun with a megaphone for a barrel. Make your commitment to the point. If you want to live a better Christian life, break it down into several specific areas where you want to improve, such as a regular prayer time, a definite Bible study program, and a positive witnessing program. Then make smaller specific commitments one at a time; be successful in one area, build on that success and add another commitment. Slowly and surely you raise the threshold of commitment and actually begin to live a more abundant Christian life.

A. Do not overcommit yourself.

Elton Trueblood, author of *The Company of the Committed* says, "Too many commitments amount virtually to none." As we make firm and specific commitments toward possibility living, the tendency is to move too fast. There is nothing worse than biting off more than you can chew and choking on the first bite. That is what often happens in a large church when a new member joins the fellowship. Invitations are extended and various types of pressure are applied for the new member to teach a Sunday School class, sing in the choir, help with the youth group, take part in home visitation, attend worship and prayer meetings, and on and on. Finally the new member is overcommitted, becomes frustrated over being spread too thin, and burns out. Then everyone wonders why the new worker suddenly disappears from the church and all his or her responsibilities.

It is better for a new member to excel at one or two things at first than to try to do too much in the beginning and fail at them all. Perhaps after the member has matured and raised the threshold of commitment, he or she can take on more commitments and greater responsibility. One commitment at a time may soon become nine, if the threshold is elevated.

B. Target the fulfillment of your commitment.

One of the conditioned reflexes most of us have is to hit the bull's-eye when a target is set before us. From childhood we have done target practice with darts, BB guns, bows and arrows, and various types of rifles and pistols. We become conditioned to hit the center of the target. Now, use that learned reflex to target the fulfillment of your commitment. Set targets or goals for your commitment and program yourself to hit the bull's-eye.

This means you answer the questions of when, where, and how much, again being firm and specific. For instance, suppose you make a commitment to read your Bible; the next step is to set a time and how often you will read it—perhaps daily, early in the morning, before breakfast. Then, decide that you will read it at the desk in your den or family room. After that, consider how much you will read—15 minutes a day or a chapter a day or three chapters a day, beginning with the Gospel of John or another favorite book.

Your commitment is now basically targeted except for a consideration of duration. If you have tried to read your Bible daily before but can't seem to stay with it for long, you might want to make the commitment for one week at first. Then you convince yourself you can surely keep it up for one week. When you are successful for a week, you get the feel of success on a short-term basis. Then building on that foundation of victory you make a slightly longer commitment and then longer and longer. That process will definitely elevate your threshold of commitment.

As you make more commitments with larger targets, there are several things you should keep in mind: (1) challenge versus attainability; (2) short-term versus long-term; and (3) your present ability versus your inherent potential.

Targets need to be a definite challenge but not beyond attainability. Your self-confidence would suffer a terrible blow if you set your first target higher than you could reach and you failed initially. On the other hand, you would not grow in self-confidence if the target were not high enough that you felt you had done more than you normally can do without special effort. Try to hit the fine balance between the two that will give you the greatest lift and get you started on the right foot.

Your targets need to be short-ranged at first. It is overwhelming to say you are going to do something every day for 10, 20 or 30 years or the rest of your life. That is why the Dale Carnegie course teaches to live in "day tight compartments" and Alcoholics Anonymous advocates, "one day at a time." Dr. Schuller teaches "inch by inch, anything is a cinch." Zig Ziglar says the way to eat an elephant is "one bite at a time." Day by day is the way. But keep in mind your long-term objectives. Today is the first day of the rest of your life; today is yesterday's tomorrow, and tomorrow will soon be today. Whatever you do today that is good for you may well be what you continue to do the rest of your life.

When setting targets, take into consideration your *present level of performance but keep an eye on your inherent potential.* Remember that you are probably not using more than 10 to 20 percent of your actual potential in any area of your life. That leaves plenty of room for growth. That superself is there below the surface still wanting to burst forth. Your targets should progressively take you from where you are to your inherent potential as you raise your threshold of commitment.

A word needs to be said here about failing. It is okay to fail at times. In fact, you will never know what your limits and potentials are unless you fail sooner or later. The only way a pole-vaulter knows how high he can vault is to finally fail at the highest level three times. The highest level which he cleared prior to failing three times was his potential at that particular time. At another time, under different circumstances, he may go higher. With more conditioning, better coaching, new and higher goals, more experience, and continued commitment he may one day vault three feet higher to reach his ultimate inherent potential. But each time he has to fail three times to know what his potential is. When you fail, you don't get discouraged. You know you are growing and reaching out. You simply pick yourself up, recommit yourself, and start over doing the best you can. When you are doing your very best, you are experiencing possibility living.

C. Establish a precise moment of commitment.

Every happily married couple can immediately tell you when they tied the knot and made their commitment to each other. Nearly every missionary can tell you when he or she was called to the mission field. Many born-again Christians can tell you the exact date that they made their commitment to Christ. Most serious runners can tell you when they started running and often how many total miles they have run in those years. Highly successful people remember their precise moment of commitment to major endeavors. This is a way you too can begin to be more successful in your personal development. Write on your commitment worksheet the date, perhaps even the hour, minute, and second when you decide to make a specific commitment. Writing the exact time to the second is not necessary, but I often do it because it makes me realize just how precious those minutes and seconds really are. If I'm going to get the most out of life, I need to use every second wisely as a good steward—it seems they aren't making them like they used to anymore. There is inflation on time as well as the dollar. Hours and minutes are still more valuable than gold, regardless of how high the market goes.

When the going gets really tough, if you know your precise moment of commitment, you can say to yourself, "I've been doing this with satisfaction for six years, why should I quit now." I have heard couples say in marriage counseling sessions, "We have been married 12 years and we don't want to give it up now." That is just one more incentive to hang in there when the going is tough, and with that attitude most couples find solutions to their problems. Knowing the moment of beginning and other information about a commitment also gives inspiration and status to your commitment. I'm sure you have seen businesses advertise, "Serving the very best prime rib at the same location for 21 years." Or, "Your Plymouth dealer since 1934." Establish your precise moment of commitment and soon you can hang out your own shingle.

D. Get a definite start.

Goethe said, "Whatever you can do, or dream you can, begin it! Boldness has genius power and magic in it." You can never win until you begin. In fact, beginning is winning. You are an automatic loser if you never start. You are over the biggest single hurdle once you start your commitment. Procrastination nips success in the seed—even before the bud stage.

Beginning is something like the lift-off of a rocket to the moon. Getting out of the earth's gravitational pull is the hard part. From then on it is mostly smooth sailing. Beginning a commitment with purpose, direction, and determination will put you into an atmosphere where success is much more easily attained.

So, you need desperately to get a definite start. I have found that a dramatic start is often a great launching pad. By dramatic I mean something special to get you moving and keep you going. Something that is impressive, enjoyable, and that you will remember as pleasant. This is especially helpful if you have had a hard time being successful at a specific commitment in the past. Let's use a commitment to stop something as an example this time, since commitments can be made to either start or stop an activity. Let's use the problem of stopping smoking after years of habitual or addictive smoking.

A definite and dramatic start in your new commitment to stop smoking might be to set a precise moment of commitment—high noon on the first of July. Your dramatic stop, which will be your start, may be to smoke your last cigarette at high noon and take that last butt and have a mock funeral for it, burying it in the ground. Imagine playing taps over the grave and then turn and walk away. I'm sure a traumatic bereavement will follow that occasion as you experience withdrawal symptoms, but the important thing is that the habit is dead and buried. Then when you crave a cigarette and are tempted to light up again, you remind yourself that the habit died as of high noon on July first.

Now that may seem a little far out to you, but the truth is, on a tough commitment such as that, you need all the help you can get. If it works, it is worth it. The object is to find ways to help you actually get started and get you turned on to success. Use your imagination in other areas of commitment. If you are starting a jogging program, you might buy yourself a colorful running outfit and good new running shoes and jog with a group of friends at a scenic location on a beautiful day. You might set up a special spot in a quiet corner with a small family altar and a couple of your favorite religious symbols to get a dramatic start for having a daily devotional time. You could get yourself a nice new modern translation of the Bible, get a bright-colored symbolic bookmark, and begin with your favorite book of the Bible to launch out on a new Bible reading commitment.

A definite start in marriage is usually rather obvious and often very dramatic. The wedding and honeymoon should be a meaningful and great beginning for a lifetime commitment. Weddings and honeymoons vary from the spectacular to the bare minimum: from colorful bridal parties in elaborate churches, elegant receptions, and resort area honeymoon suites to a couple and their witnesses at the courthouse and a steal-away honeymoon. There is no correlation between the expense or elaborateness of the wedding and honeymoon and the quality of the marriage, but there is definitely a correlation between how seriously the couple sees the wedding and the honeymoon as the beginning of a lifetime commitment and the depth of the marriage. When two people openly and publicly pledge themselves to each other in unconditional commitment in the presence of God and witnesses, they have dramatically started on the right foot. That start will constantly be in their memory as the beginning of an adventure for better or for worse, for richer or for poorer, in sickness and in health, till death shall part them.

Just how definite and how dramatic you make your start in your commitment depends upon your own preference and your imagination, but do get a positive start. If in the past you have been conservative and shunned dramatic activity, perhaps now is the time to change your style. A little drama may save a lot of trauma in the long run.

E. Let yourself get excited about your commitment.

This step is very carefully worded to say "let" yourself get excited, because that is precisely one of our problems. Most people have a natural tendency to get excited about what they are involved in, but after a period of exposure to the elements of society they withdraw and lose their enthusiasm.

When we get excited about something, we face so much criticism and negativism that we learn never to "let" ourselves get excited, to keep from being criticized. I tend to get excited very easily about a lot of things I am involved in. I've been criticized and given strange looks for getting so excited. I've been told by close friends that they wish I would react to things like "normal" people and not get so carried away. Most negative thinkers just don't like to see people get as positive and enthusiastic as I do. Consequently they lash out, and it hurts a little to be criticized so we withdraw and lose the ability to get excited. My friend, there is nothing wrong with getting excited about being successful and doing great things.

George Washington Carver said, "When you do the common things of life in an uncommon way, you will command the attention of the world." That is exactly what you are doing when you are doing God's will, serving others, and becoming what you were created to be—through commitment. That is abundant life, that is possibility living, and that is exciting! Honest and heartfelt excitement and enthusiasm will take you a long way toward the fulfillment of your commitment.

Wow! With all that adrenaline flowing, let's move on to the third *C*.

7

Step 3—Coordinate All Your Resources Toward Your Targets

*My help comes from the
Lord, who made heaven and earth.*
Psalm 121:2

The psalmist was wise when he said, "From whence shall my help come? My help comes from the Lord, who made heaven and earth" (Ps. 121:1,2). First, he was wise enough to seek help: he asked where his help would come from. Secondly, he was wise enough to accept help: he acknowledged where his help came from. Thirdly, he was wise in recognizing his greatest source of help: God. This is the kind of wisdom we need to capture in carrying out our commitments.

It has often been said that no man is an island. No one stands alone, and no one succeeds alone—not even Mohammed Ali, the outstanding athlete of the decade of the '70s. Ali seemed to be a one-man three-ring circus, winning the world heavyweight championship three times. He is fighter, movie actor, television personality, and even a children's cartoon character. But he didn't do it all alone, even though no one else was in the ring with him but his opponent and the referee. Many people helped him become what he is and do what he did—trainers, managers, promoters, partners, directors, sportscasters, family, friends, and you and me. His task was that of coordinating his own abilities, with the assistance of others, to carry out his aspirations and to reach his possibilities.

No one carries out a commitment alone either. Just as a gear can't turn a mill alone, a flute player can't perform an opera by himself, and a bricklayer can't build a building without the help of the carpenter, electrician, and plumber, so we can't carry out our commitments by ourselves. We need to be managers, coordinating all our resources toward the completion or carrying out of our commitments. There are many resources available to you. You just need to get them all going in the same direction: toward your targets. It is amazing what you can do if you can get enough momentum. I've heard that you could drive a wet noodle through a plate of steel if you could just get it going fast enough. Get all your resources moving out and you can pierce great obstacles.

A. Develop and focus your own resources.

We have already talked about your fantastic inherent potential. You have abilities and powers you never even dared dream about. You now, as a wise manager, begin to develop that potential by applying yourself to your targets and game plan. You focus your best efforts toward the target just like you can focus the sun on a piece of paper with a magnifying glass and burn a hole in the paper. You can get on fire and accomplish great things!

It is precisely here, at the point of focus, where you really begin to raise your threshold of commitment and live your possibilities. Here is where you do your thing and begin to grow. You will actually begin to accomplish more than you have ever accomplished before if your targets are challenging. As you make progress, you begin to feel better about yourself, have more, do more, and be more than ever before. You will like the new you and the great possibility living adventure will be well on its way.

B. Ask for and utilize help from others.

To try to climb a dangerous mountain peak all alone the first time out as a climber would be purely insane. There are hundreds of people who would gladly help you accomplish your goal if you would only seek their help. No great commitment should be attempted without the assistance of others.

There are individuals, clubs, professional groups, and organizations of all types whose purpose is to assist, encourage, and provide information on just about every area of accomplishment imaginable. Take mountain climbing as we just mentioned. There are many mountain-climbing and back-packing clubs, many books published on the subject, many climbing schools, and numerous experienced individuals who can lend invaluable assistance. Help is on the way if you only ask for it and utilize it.

But often we are too proud or stubborn and want to go it alone and do not ask for help. I have suffered several rather serious running injuries through the years, and each time I first tried to solve them myself. But each time I was unsuccessful until I went to others for help. My first injury was an Achilles tendon problem. I very modestly sought help from local resources several times but received no relief. Then I finally went to an authority. Through a friend who is certified as an aerobic counselor by Dr. Kenneth Cooper's Aerobic Center in Dallas, Texas, I found the solution. Kenneth Cooper developed the entire concept of aerobic exercises and introduced the world to this extremely popular and important activity in his first book in 1968. Of course, he would have the answer; which brings us to an important point—don't be afraid to ask important people for help. Go to the authorities for the greatest source of help. They may be extremely busy and may not be able to give you personal attention, but they will see that you receive assistance. They want to help you be successful because they are interested in success in their field of expertise.

One of the primary functions of the church is to help you to be successful in your Christian commitments. The fellowship is to encourage, to teach, to pray for one another, and to work together to do God's will. The church and its leaders publish books, provide training courses, colleges, universities, seminaries, and a multitude of other institutions and agencies to help you carry out your commitments. Even foreign and home mission boards or societies exist primarily to assist those who have made a commitment to mission work to be successful in their calling and commitment. To fail to use these vast resources is to miss tremendous opportunity for growth and to flirt with failure.

Do others a favor, ask them to help you. It will give them an opportunity to serve and help you carry out your commitment.

Often, however, you will not know the right people to ask for help and they will not know you need help, so make your commitment public. If you keep your commitment a secret, it is almost certain to be doomed to failure. If you let it be known what you are attempting, people will volunteer to help you. If your commitment is a beautiful idea, people will seek you out and ask to have a part in the carrying out of your commitment.

But perhaps even more importantly, if you keep your commitment a secret, if you fail, nobody will know about it but you. That is setting up a built-in failure mechanism. You are admitting possible failure and lack of self-confidence from the beginning if you keep the commitment a secret. Announce your intentions publicly and you are showing your confidence in your own success, plus putting your reputation on the line. You will put pressure on yourself which will be a tremendous incentive to continue your commitment when you feel like quitting.

If you are attempting a commitment at which you failed in the past, or doing something that is very difficult or seems impossible, tell everybody about it. Shout it from the mountaintops! People will come from everywhere to support you. They will pull for you, pray for you, and pressure you—and you will be successful!

One of my greatest personal achievements was a result of my publicly stating my intentions. I made a commitment to run the White Rock Marathon in Dallas, Texas, on December 3, 1977. As you probably know, a full marathon is 26 miles and 385 yards. For a 45-year-old amateur runner, that is a long way. I got so excited about it that I told all my running friends, all my co-workers, family, and everybody else I could get to listen that I was going to run the marathon.

Many of my running buddies were there that day and I was really psyched up. I did nearly everything right except I made the almost fatal mistake of parking my van near the start/finish line so I could change shoes if I began to develop blisters. The course was three laps on an 8.7-mile course, and I unwisely decided that a break after each lap to freshen up and perhaps change shoes would be good.

Things went well the first 8.7 miles. I took a short break and had some quick-energy drink and took off again in fine shape. After the second lap at about 17.5 miles I stopped at the van again and sat down to change shoes. About that time a fellow runner in the van next to me announced to me that he was quitting. That hit a familiar chord for I was thinking the same thing. After changing shoes, I began to feel like quitting and just sitting there. When I started to get up, I could hardly move. I was cooling off and getting stiff, both physically and mentally.

Then it hit me like a bolt of greased lightning. I had told all my friends I was going to finish this marathon! I thought of how many of them were pulling for me, even some praying I'd be able to do it. Then I thought of how I would feel Monday morning telling them I had quit. That did it. I suddenly bounced up and hit the road. By then I had gotten sore and couldn't run continuously, so I alternately walked and ran the last 8.7 miles—and I finished! Many earlier finishers and spectators cheered me on as I "sprinted" across the finish line with the last bit of energy I had.

My time was very slow at 4 hours, 39 minutes and 58 seconds, but I had completed my commitment. I had finished a marathon! I had never felt so much confidence and such a wonderful sense of accomplishment. When I crossed the finish line, I was so totally exhausted I had to sit down and lean on a post but I felt great inside. I was able to complete the commitment only because I had made it public. Thank you, friends!

Finishing a marathon was not only a great physical and psychological experience for me, but it was also a wonderful religious experience. It showed me how great God was when He created man and what wonderful strength He gave to us. It showed me that God had made me to excel and to grow. I had tasted of just a part of my inherent potential and it was fantastic. I was filled with wonder, joy, and reverence as I realized I had experienced Isaiah 40:31, "Yet those who wait for the Lord will gain new strength; they will mount up with wings like eagles, they will run and not get tired, they will walk and not become weary."

Making your commitment public is very important in the Christian life. I cannot imagine a genuine Christian who does not in some way make his commitment to Christ public. Even the Christians under Roman persecutions, at the threat of death, made their commitment known. Many evangelical churches give new Christians an opportunity to publicly confess Christ; some may even require a public confession and commitment to Christ in a worship service. All churches have some form of public declaration, either at a confirmation or baptism or similar occasion. When Christ said, "Every one therefore who shall confess Me before men, I will also confess him before My Father who is in heaven" (Matt. 10:32), He substantiated the need for a public commitment. When the new Christian makes his commitment public, fellow Christians can encourage the new member, help him, pray for him, and work together to help him grow in his commitment.

C. Seek and accept God's help.

To try to be a success in life and share in possibility living through commitment without relying on God would be like trying to mow the lawn with an electric mower that isn't plugged in. Oh, you would tear a few blades of grass off and bend some over with the wheels and the motionless blade, but you would miss the main source of power and assistance without any electricity.

I'm a Texas Aggie and have been the brunt of many an Aggie joke through the years. They used to bother me a little at times but finally I decided, "If I can't whip 'em, join 'em," so I just join in and tell the jokes too. One of my favorites is about the Aggie who bought a new heavy-duty chain saw that was guaranteed to cut three cords of firewood a day. After several days of hard labor with the saw he brought it back to the dealer. He complained that it would only cut one cord a day and asked to have it checked out. The dealer took it and pulled the start rope to test it out and it started immediately. Suddenly the Aggie got wide-eyed, jumped back, and said, "Where is all that noise coming from?"

Our lives are often like that when we try to live without the Spirit of God at work in us. We work hard, trying to carry all the burden ourselves and make little progress. If we will turn Him on in our lives and let Him work through us, we can do amazing things. With God we can dream big dreams, make big commitments, and accomplish big tasks. Jesus said, "With God all things are possible" (Matt. 19:26).

Of course, there are many ways to receive God's help and power in your life, but most basic is to commit yourself to Him in a very specific commitment of faith and then live close to Him in your daily walk of life. Open yourself to the power of the Holy Spirit at work within you and pray fervently that His will might be done through you. God will help you to be successful and to develop your inherent potential because He created you to excel. He will help you to carry out your specific commitments if you will only seek and accept His help. He is concerned with the smallest detail of your life. He loves you and wants you to grow and bear fruit.

So, don't be stubborn and try to go it alone. Be a good manager and coordinate all your resources: your own abilities, the help of others, and the power of God. Then you will have extra strength to stay with the commitment until the fruit is mature—which is the fourth C.

8
Step 4—Complete Your Commitment

And the seed in the good ground, these are the ones who have heard the word in an honest and good heart, and hold it fast, and bear fruit with perseverance.
Luke 8:15

Have you ever tried eating grapes that are only half mature, before they get ripe? It is a bitter experience! But give them a little more time and they become tasty and sweet. Commitments are like that. If you quit halfway through, it is a bitter experience of failure. Stay with it a little longer and it will be an enjoyable, sweet success.

In the parable of the sower, Christ tells of four kinds of soil in which seeds are sown. The first is the soil beside the road where the seeds are trampled under foot and the birds of the air devour them. The second type of soil is rocky ground and, as soon as the seeds grow up, they wither away because there is no moisture. The third is among the thorns where, as the seeds grow, they are choked out by the thorns. The last soil is good ground. Here the seeds grow and produce fruit a hundredfold.

Christ interpreted this parable to the apostles as a parable about the Word of God. But when you look at the parable from the perspective of the soil or those who receive the Word, it is a parable about commitment. Only those who are totally committed to the Word, "and hold it fast . . . bear fruit with perseverance."

The clincher is, hang in there until the job is done! But it can be done. Thousands and even millions before you have been successful and fulfilled their commitments. There are several important points that will help you be successful in fulfilling your commitment.

A. Give the commitment enough time to bear fruit.

Perhaps the greatest downfall in success is quitting your commitment before it has had time to bring any results. Perseverance is most often the weak link in the chain to possibility living. Every commitment has to have a period of time before it will bring forth any fruit, just as a seed must have time to mature and bring forth a harvest. If you quit a commitment halfway through, you will experience a bitter failure. Stay with the commitment a little longer and you will reap a bountiful harvest of success.

The growing cycle or gestation period of a particular commitment is totally dependent upon the nature of the commitment. The duration could be from minutes to a lifetime. It usually takes much more time to harvest the results than we would like. Many times we lack patience to see it through, and consequently we suffer a frustrating experience of failure.

What happens, for instance, if you go on a strict diet for a week? You hurt a lot—hunger pains, weakness, the discipline of saying no. You may only lose a few pounds and those will come back as soon as you get off the diet. You must stay with it long enough to lose enough to get a new pair of pants or a new skirt and to begin to have people say you look nice. You have to stay with it long enough to begin to feel better about yourself. To lose weight just to gain it back over and over is just a visit to frustration city.

Even a business commitment does not normally bear any fruit the first year. Many new business ventures lose money the first year. The next years are hard work and only several years down the road does the business really begin to show a profit. The same principle holds true of professions, skilled vocations, and the ministry. A minister or missionary often does not make much progress the first few years after seminary training. Only when he or she sticks with the commitment long enough will he or she begin to reap the true harvest.

So, in setting your goals and targets, consider well the time frame and the fruit-bearing cycle and commit yourself to the perseverance of the commitment. Once you have learned this lesson and begin to raise the threshold of commitment and bring in the fruit, you will want to become a truck farmer. It is the sweet taste of success that will keep you going.

B. Stop the commitment only when you complete it or it becomes destructive.

"Do not quit" seems to be indelibly etched on the whole being of successful people. "Winners never quit and quitters never win." Quitting is very destructive to your self-confidence. You were made to succeed and when you quit you are less than your real self. If you do fail, do not quit. Get up and start over, because it may be that you have to fail several times before you are finally successful. So keep on keeping on, don't give up, press on, and every moment you hang in there your threshold will rise and you will grow.

Some time ago Dr. Robert Schuller faced a very difficult phase of his ministry when his congregation was divided about whether he should build the first walk-in-drive-in sanctuary. He stated that he was depressed and often thought he would be happy if somehow, by an act of God, he could be relieved of all responsibility. But instead of quitting and failing, he chose to succeed. He sat down and wrote a commitment to himself which today is known as the Possibility Thinker's Creed. He wrote, "When faced with a mountain, I will not quit. I will keep on striving until I climb over, find a path through, tunnel underneath—or simply stay and turn the mountain into a gold mine with God's help!" As you well know, he did not quit, and the sanctuary was built, as was the Tower of Hope, and now the Crystal Cathedral. That creed has been an inspiration to millions—including myself—as it is now printed on posters, postcards, and the Possibility Thinker's medallion. I carry one of the medallions with me all the time as a reminder never to quit, even when it looks hopeless.

Never quit until your commitment is completed, and even then you may want to recommit yourself and continue on. Many commitments do have a definite point of completion, such as reading a book, climbing a mountain or painting a picture. Other commitments continue indefinitely or are lifelong, such as the Christian commitment or marriage. Even if a specific commitment is completed, such as taking a continuing education course, you might continue your commitment and take another course, if the first one was profitable to you. If a particular commitment is finished and you do not want to continue in that area, you should find another commitment to take its place so that you will keep growing upward.

If in the process of completing a commitment, harm or destruction of any kind is done to you, others, or the Kingdom of God, you probably should stop the commitment. However, before stopping, critically analyze what is happening. For instance, if you are considering abandoning an activity because it has become a burden and is leaving you tired, drained, and depressed, look seriously at what might be causing your negative feelings. If your depression is because you are not progressing as you would like, perhaps you are not giving it your very best effort. It could be that what you really need, instead of quitting, is a recommitment with greater drive.

If the commitment is harming your health, being destructive to your family relationships, or is a poor witness for Christ, stop immediately or modify the commitment to alleviate the harm. If new information is learned about your commitment that changes the picture from what it was when you chose the commitment in step 1, stop and regroup. An example of why this may be necessary can be found in many of the modern diets that are frequently proposed. Often, after further research, it is found that something about a particular diet is actually harmful to health. In this case, if you are following this diet, stop the commitment and begin searching for a new diet that has been proven to be satisfactory.

While fulfilling a commitment, you cannot simply stop when you experience hurt or pain. If you stopped every time you faced discomfort, you would never grow. There is some type of hurt, pain, or sacrifice required for every worthwhile commitment in which you grow and experience the fullness of life. It is a universal principle that there is no growth without pain and there is no gain without strain. As an example, what happens when you are on a strict diet that includes no sweets and someone offers you a big dish of your favorite "yummie" at a party? If you stick to your commitment, you will have to say, "No, thanks," and that will hurt in more ways than one. But from the "no," you will grow, and you will finally bear the fruit of loss of weight. Many of us are not willing to hurt enough to be successful in life.

Every athlete has to learn to hurt to be competitive. Marathon runners often run for miles with blisters on their feet; a gymnast continues a routine without a flaw after he tears a hand on the highbar; a boxer goes five more rounds with his eyes almost swollen shut and with a broken rib; or a bicycle racer sprints to the finish line for first place with every muscle ready to explode from being pushed to the limit.

When Roger Bannister broke the four-minute mile the first time, he said that after crossing the finish line he collapsed almost unconscious and "felt like an exploding flashlight with no will to live." But after the announcer stated that his time was 3 minutes 59.4 seconds, he said he experienced "spontaneous joy." He describes the feeling in his book, *First Four Minutes*: "No words could be invented for such supreme happiness, eclipsing all other feelings. I thought at that moment I could never again reach such a climax of single-mindedness."

When I crossed the finish line at the White Rock Marathon, I hurt like I had never hurt before. It was the feeling of total depletion from head to toe. At the same time, though, I never felt a higher moment of satisfaction, growth and fullness of life. It was a sweet mixture of agony and ecstasy at the same time. In fact, I think there needs to be a new word in the English language to describe this feeling. The word should be *agasy*. This agasy is a feeling that only they who want to grow and are not afraid to risk a little to do so will ever experience. It is a wonderful feeling. It is living on the cutting edge of growth. It is possibility living.

There is also no gain without strain, which simply means you must extend yourself to improve yourself. A weight lifter never becomes a champion without straining his muscles to their limit day after day until he grows to the level of strength he desires or reaches his maximum potential. The educator does not expand his knowledge by reading simple books on things he already knows about. He or she must venture into more challenging literature, do research, or get field experience to expand and stretch the mental capacity. The Christian does not grow in stewardship by giving the same small amount to the same cause all the time. He must meet new challenges and give until it strains the budget; then comes the blessing and the growth.

It is here at the point of strain and pain that the threshold of commitment and the threshold of pain run parallel. If you have a low threshold of pain, you cry ouch at the earliest sign of pain or strain and seek to rid yourself of whatever is the cause of the discomfort. If the threshold of pain is higher, you can tolerate the pain longer without withdrawing. If you have a low threshold of commitment, you will break your commitment as soon as the first bit of discomfort appears. Of course, that will cause even deeper pain because you suffer a defeat which scars your self-confidence. If you develop a high threshold of commitment, you will actually learn to tolerate and enjoy pain because you know you are growing. After this principle is mastered, you will even long to hurt a little to experience the growth that accompanies the strain and the pain.

The pain and the hurts are a reality. They are there when you discipline yourself to a task as a result of a firm and specific commitment. But every hurt is worthwhile when progress is made and you get ahead and become a better person from fulfilling a commitment. The pain and strain are well worth the gain. The paradise is worth the sacrifice.

C. Quit a commitment only with a rational decision.

In step 1 you made a rational decision to start your commitment. In step 2 you rationally set targets and began your commitment. Now, do not quit your commitment as a result of rationalization or irrational thought. If you do quit, it must be as a result of a process of rational thought.

For instance, do not say, "I'll study my Bible and pray when I'm a little older; I'm too busy having fun right now." Or, "It will be easier to lose weight next summer; I'll wait." You can always rationalize a better time, but in reality the present is the only time we have. Do it now or never.

A young man who worked in my office told me one day, "I'm going to stop smoking right now," and he threw his cigarettes in the trash can. The next day he was smoking again. I asked him what happened. He said, "I decided I'll wait until basketball season starts and then I'll go work out hard and get real sick because I'm so out of shape, then I'll quit." With thoughts like that, I'm afraid he is more likely to quit basketball than smoking.

Don't let your momentary negative emotional feelings cause you to stop your commitment either. Sometimes we have a bad day or a series of bad experiences that cause us to feel low, but don't let that bring on more negative feelings by becoming a quitter. When negative feelings creep in, reaffirm your commitment and give it your very best effort and your feelings will turn upward as you make new progress.

If you made a right decision in choosing your commitment, do not quit as long as that decision is valid. At any time you rationally decide you should stop a commitment for some specific reason, you may stop. If, for instance, you learn additional facts that cause you to change your mind, you might quit your commitment or alter it to meet your new criteria. Do not quit your commitment as long as step 1 is still valid.

D. Enjoy your commitment.

I thoroughly believe if all the evidence were fed into a master computer, we would find that man was created and put on this earth to enjoy life. Not that enjoyment is his sole purpose or that it is most important, but I believe God wants us to be happy and joyful. I think we would also find, if all the evidence were in, that we were created to live a committed life. Further, I am convinced that enough evidence is available to conclude that the key to happiness and abundant life is through commitment to great ideas and great causes, commitment to living as

God has created us to live. We might put it this way: Commitment to excellence, both physical and spiritual, is possibility living—and that brings joy.

So, enjoy your commitment. Enjoy the fruit of the committed life. Enjoy seeing others' needs fulfilled as you bring forth a harvest. Enjoy deeper relationships with God and your fellowman through commitments that build trust and mutual love and respect. Enjoy seeing your community and nation grow as you commit yourself to doing more than your part to make it a great place to live. Enjoy seeing yourself grow and mature as you build personal character, better health, and a deeper spiritual life.

Well, there you have it, the 4 C's and their sub-steps in the process of commitment. There is nothing magical about it, but it works. The whole process is simple, straightforward, practical and easy to follow if you are genuinely interested in getting more out of your life. The process is just like everything else in life, it will only work if you use it. Someone could develop an absolutely foolproof pill to cure all illnesses and package it in the most beautiful, easy-open bottle you ever saw, but it would cure none of your diseases unless you opened the bottle and took the pill.

To make it easier to swallow the sweet pill of success, chapter 9 gives some guidance in tracking your new commitments.

9

Tracking Your Commitment

*For the gate is small, and
the way is narrow that
leads to life, and few are
those who find it.*
Matthew 7:14

In the early pioneer days, the days of covered wagons and wagon trains, a scout was a necessity. The well-experienced scout knew where the wagon train was at all times, because he knew where the travelers had been and where they were going. He would get the wagons to their destination because he had a plan and a program. He had direction!

A very small percent of twentieth-century individuals actually get out of life what they desire. Some studies indicate that as low as three percent of Americans reach the level of success they aspire to in life. Many of those 97 percent who fall short do so because they don't know where they have been or where they are going.

Jesus Christ said the passage is narrow that leads to eternal life and few enter in. So is the gate to success and few enter in. But the gate to success can be navigated with confidence if you have a plan and a program, just as salvation is assured if you follow the scriptural plan of salvation. You can enter the realm of success if you have your own personal, proven, and experienced scout.

Your "scout" is found in chapter 12 and is called "Your Threshold of Commitment Workbook." First there is a bibliography of both books and tapes which can be a tremendous inspiration and a real source of information to help you raise your threshold. Second, there is an outline of the steps of commitment and their sub-steps. This provides you with a handy outline of the full process of commitment so that you may easily review them as you write out your commitments on the worksheets. Last, there are 10 "Steps of Commitment Worksheets" which can be the practical day-by-day heart of your new program to reach your possibilities. Read from the books and listen to the tapes listed and learn the process of commitment. Then use the commitment worksheets to the letter and they will guide you to your possibilities. You can either (1) use this book with the sheets intact as your workbook; (2) tear out the sheets and put them in a loose-leaf notebook; or (3) duplicate the pages and make a separate workbook, adding commitment sheets as you elevate your threshold of commitment.

The top portion of the worksheet lists the 4 C's as a quick reminder of the process as you use the sheets. The remainder of the worksheet gives you an opportunity to put your commitment in writing and visually track its progress to completion. Business and industry spend millions of dollars in tracking their interests to completion and success. Add this time-tested method to your personal life at no cost and watch your progress.

You can use a worksheet in any and every commitment you make, but you should especially use one in its entirety in areas where you have been ineffective and need all the help you can get. The worksheet's greatest virtue is that it is in writing. Writing out your commitment does wonders. It clarifies what you want to do, be, or have like no other method. It puts your commitment in black and white, out in the open where you can see it and it can become concrete. Often commitments are intangible.

They need to be thought out and put on paper, even if very briefly. The three percent of Americans who have written goals for their lives out-perform by 10 to 100 times those who have no written goals. If you write out your commitment and your goals and then track them to their completion, you could multiply even those impressive statistics.

I personally keep a bound notebook of my commitment worksheets on my desk at all times. I have 25 or so worksheets in it, some completed, others at various stages of growth. I also keep a short journal in the back of the notebook and make daily notes of my progress in various commitments, so I know at all times my own personal progress. From time to time I review my current commitments and post progress reports on the bottom. I often continue progress reports on another sheet of paper if the worksheet is filled up.

I never let this system get to be a burden. That is why it is simple and straightforward. If a tracking system is complicated and troublesome, you are much more likely to abandon it and add another frustrating failure to your list. I seldom take more than a couple of minutes per day jotting in activities of the day and then 10 or 15 minutes periodically reviewing and updating various commitments. But the very fact that my personal "Threshold of Commitment Workbook" is on my desk is a constant reminder of where I am going and the progress I am making. It is like having my own personal scout right at hand anytime I start to stray from the trail to the west. Life is too short and precious to waste it wandering aimlessly in the desert when you could be on the path of success climbing to exciting elevations of progress. That's why I keep my scout close by.

Now, let's look at that commitment worksheet and learn how to make it work for you. First, notice in the upper left-hand corner is the Threshold of Commitment symbol.

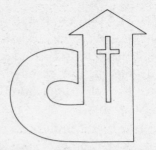

The *C* is a visual reminder that commitment is the master key to success in your life. The arrow pointing upward indicates that the threshold of commitment can be raised, lifting you to new heights of achievement. The cross in the center of the arrow symbolizes the inspiration and strength available to you in your upward journey.

I am a firm believer in symbols. Symbols can be great inspirations and great motivators. For centuries and millenniums armies have marched behind symbols of their country, their cause, and their God. Millions have willingly given their lives and their all for their flag. The symbol of commitment is added inspiration to conquer failure and be victorious in possibility living.

Now, look at the 4 C's of commitment.

1. *CHOOSE* YOUR COMMITMENT WISELY
2. *COMMIT* YOURSELF FIRMLY AND SPECIFICALLY
3. *COORDINATE* ALL YOUR RESOURCES TOWARD YOUR TARGETS
4. *COMPLETE* YOUR COMMITMENT

Each time I make a commitment, I go through every step and sub-step, one by one, and actually follow the full process mentally with that commitment. I visualize, plan, imagine, plot, and project myself through the whole cycle each time. As I go through the 4 C's, I often write answers to the questions in the sub-steps, make notes, write reminders, and even write myself pep talks in the blank spaces between the four steps.

After you have reviewed the 4 C's, then move to the lined portion of the sheet. First, write out your commitment.

My commitment is _____

_____

The simpler and more direct, the better. Your commitment should normally be one sentence, probably beginning with "to"—to be something, to do something, or to have something. For instance, your commitment might be "to become a Bible teacher," or "to write a poem," or "to get a new car." Keeping it short and to the point puts your commitment right out where it can be easily grasped. This step alone is a tremendous step forward in your personal success. The minute you put it in writing you join the three percent who out-perform everyone else by 10 to 100 times. This is a part of your definite start toward raising your threshold of commitment.

But don't stop there. Move right along. Write out your targets as we discussed in B of step 2 in chapter 6. Again be brief and to the point, yet comprehensive enough to give you guidance and direction as to what, how much, when, where, and how you will carry out the commitment. This is your road map to your destination and your checklist as to how you are going to get there.

My targets are _____

_____

_____

_____

_____

_____

_____

Next on the worksheet is the precise moment of commitment. Check the calendar and your watch and write in the date and the time. We have discussed this in detail in chapter 6, Step 2, under section C. Putting the time in writing in your tracking workbook and reviewing it regularly will give you a sense of where you have been and how long you have been at it. This will help you get an idea of your position in the fruit-bearing cycle of the commitment. It will help you to keep on keeping on.

My precise moment of commitment is _____

I often look back at the date of the beginning of my commitment to aerobic running, October 21, 1968, with fond memories of that rather distant historic moment in the growth of my life. I think about the many years of pleasant runs and I feel great about it all. It reminds me of all the challenging competitive runs I've participated in with my friends, and I get lifted up in a little of the ecstasy of commitment. And I'm not about to quit now and stop the chain of all those great years! No, sir! It gets more interesting each year. I can imagine looking at that old worn and faded logbook when I'm 87 years old and rejoicing over the 50 years of fun on the run. I may not be able to see the old logbook very well when I'm 97, but it won't be because I didn't get enough exercise or think positively about it.

Next on the "Steps of Commitment Worksheet" comes perhaps the most important line on the sheet, your signature. Sign your commitment with the same seriousness as someone might sign a treaty or a pact with his own blood. This is serious business. You are dealing with your personal potential, your future, your success. Again it's not the burdensome kind of serious, but the enjoyable kind. Of course, there is nothing legal or negotiable about this signature. It is simply a pledge of the sincerity of your commitment. It is your personal seal to yourself that you mean business and you are going to do what you decided you want to do and ought to do in the choosing phase of step 1. If you don't mean it, don't sign it! But sign it and you have bought it, and you can do it!

Next comes your definite start. Notice that it is in the past tense, "was." After you have started, write out in a brief sentence or two how you started, whether it was very dramatic or not. The fact that it is in the past tense confirms that you have now made your definite beginning. Remember, beginning is half done. Now that you are started, you are on your way to an exciting adventure of achievement.

My definite start was _____

_____

_____

Move on down now to your progress reports. Here you keep short notes on your milestones of achievement. This can be done as regularly as you feel is profitable. It could be weekly, daily, or monthly, depending on the length of your commitment, the amount of measurable progress, and your personal desire. On some long-term commitments I make notes of progress only every couple of months. I often write notes here when I review all of my commitments. I might just jot down, "still doing okay, Jan. 3, '81." I sometimes go back and review all the short progress reports to see how growth toward the target is progressing and how I'm getting to where I want to go.

Progress reports: _____

_____

_____

_____

_____

When your commitment is completed, the last thing on the sheet is to check the completed box and put in the date of completion. This will serve to help you track your many commitments and visually see your progress. The more commitments you check off and complete, the more fruitful your life is; and the more you accomplish, the more abundance of life you reap.

Some commitments, of course, you will never complete. Some commitments as we already know are lifetime. (So someone else may have to check off your lifetime commitments after you have gone to your just reward.) Some commitments may take years to complete, or a decade or more. That is why I recommend that you begin by making commitments that are short-ranged and can be completed in a reasonable time frame in order to raise your threshold of commitment immediately. The first few should perhaps require only a few days or weeks to complete. That gets the process moving and turns the threshold upward immediately.

Okay now, "head 'em up and move 'em out." Your own personal scout is now ready to lead you on a new venture through the straight and narrow trail that leads to a new frontier of success.

10
You *Can* Raise Your Threshold of Commitment

*I can do all things through
Him who strengthens me.*
Philippians 4:13

Perhaps the strongest affirmation in the English language is "I can." One of the most destructive statements is "I can't." Usually achievement has almost nothing to do with talent, abilities, or resources. It is a battle of the will or attitude. Spinoza said, "As long as man imagines that he cannot do a certain thing . . . it is impossible for him to do it." Someone else said, "Success is more attitude than aptitude." A beautiful poster with sea gulls in full flight has the words, "They can because they think they can," boldly printed on the blue sky. Decide you can, and you will.

The apostle Paul's most positive affirmation is found in his letter to the Philippians. He says, "I can do all things through Him who strengthens me" (4:13). That bold statement of faith in Christ was proven true in his life of fantastic success even amidst hardships of all kinds. Paul was a winner in the truest sense because he believed in himself and his potential in Christ. At times Paul almost sounded boastful in his writing, but he was only showing positive affirmation of his ability to succeed in the service God called him to perform. It is not bragging if you can do what you say you can. It is a statement of fact. Paul simply recognized his potential and in union with Christ he developed it, and the world has never been the same since.

Do your realize that you could be just as successful and as strong as Paul the apostle? Of course, you could! "But," you say, "he was an extraordinary person." Not so! He was an ordinary person just like you and me. He put his toga on one arm at a time like everybody else. In fact, he didn't have all the advantages of a modern age as we do. But Paul did have extraordinary commitment, and his commitment gave him great energy and drive to carry out his dreams of spreading the gospel across the lands. He just said, "I can," and he did. And you can too!

Using the steps of commitment as we have outlined, you can raise your threshold of commitment higher and higher until you can reach your possibilities! You too can be fully successful, even if you have always considered yourself a failure.

Okay, let's face it. Perhaps you have been a failure at times. All of us have. Sometimes we even seem to fail time after time. You may even consider yourself a real loser. Well, guess what? You may feel like a loser, but you are not, and there is no reason to feel that way. Just because you have not always succeeded doesn't make you a loser. It doesn't mean you can't succeed either. Everyone can succeed. It is a matter of attitude and commitment.

Let's look at your attitude for a minute. From the Old Testament Proverbs to hundreds of psychologists, motivational experts, theologians, and human engineers of our times, the truth is, "As a man thinks, so is he" (see Prov. 23:7). Fact: you are a product of your attitude. Zig Ziglar says some of us have "hardening of the attitudes," and it is true. We are often locked into our attitude about ourselves, and we don't want to change.

Your life can change if your attitude changes. Attitudes can be changed as quickly as a suit of clothes, or quicker. Attitudes are not inherited, or pressed on us, or out of the blue. They are chosen by us.

Zig Ziglar also says he made up his mind years ago that he was going to feel good and he has felt good ever since. You can change your attitude simply by wanting to, and doing it. It is a process of mental discipline and decision. You can change from "I can't" to "I can" as quickly as you can read this line.

But you say, "I can't change my feelings about myself." Can you change your mind about going out for an evening of entertainment? Of course, you can! So you can change your feelings about yourself because your thought processes govern your feelings and you govern your thought processes. If you can purposely think in your mind right now the number "1," you can control your thought process. Think "I can" and you can.

With a change of attitude must come action. Success is not measured in material things but is measured in action, both mental and physical. There is a tremendous emphasis on action in the Scriptures. God created man to perform—to do, to become, to serve, to live. This is where commitment comes into the picture. "I can" by itself is passive, but "I can" with commitment is action. For instance, James in his New Testament letter says, "Even so faith, if it has no works, is dead, being by itself . . .; show me your faith without the works, and I will show you my faith by my works" (2:17,18). It is not enough just to "believe"; James goes on to say that the "demons also believe, and shudder" (2:19). You certainly won't find any demons doing good works and living for Christ. Of course not, because there is no commitment along with their belief. A person who believes deeply enough to add a positive commitment to Christ to his faith will become a new creation and bring forth fruits of action a hundredfold. Add commitment to your positive mental attitude and you are a winner. You are on your way to success.

I'm sure, however, that our naturally negative minds will find reasons why we can't put action to our positive attitude. You may already be thinking, "That all sounds great, but I've tried before and it didn't work." You may be saying, "I've been positive before but I can't actually seem to do what I want to do. My spirit is willing but my flesh is weak."

This is a common problem that all of us struggle with. We call it lack of *willpower*. Willpower is the drive to perform what we should do or want to do. In actuality, what we are saying is that we don't have control over our physical bodies. Let's do an almost silly little exercise right now. Take your right hand and hold it in front of you. Now, open your hand wide. Now close it into a fist and clinch it tightly. Do that three times in a row. That wasn't hard at all was it? Well, if you can do that simple exercise, it means you have control over your body, unless you have paralysis or some type of physical or neurological condition which limits your physical activity.

I learned as a young boy that the normally healthy person can control his or her body and do whatever he or she wants simply by acting. I was raised at a cotton gin since my father was the manager of a local gin. As boys we spent hours playing on the bales of cotton and the boxcars on the railroad switch track next to the cotton platform behind the gin. One of our favorite tricks was to jump off the boxcars onto the bales of cotton. Like Superman, I would almost fly. I remember well when I was about 10 years old, I started to jump to a bale but my perception told me the jump was a bit farther than usual and would be a bit harder. At the same time I felt a little afraid and hesitant. My mind told me, "I can make it," but my emotions were apprehensive. I studied the situation a moment and decided, "I can if I want to." So I exercised mind over body and jumped. I vividly remember the thrill of the long "flight" and I made it with room to spare. It was exciting! I learned then and there that the mind controls the body. As a boy of 10 years of age I was practicing Napoleon Hill's statement, "Whatever the mind of man can conceive and believe, it can achieve."

Willpower and self-confidence are very closely akin. Often we lack willpower because we suffer low self-esteem and self-confidence. Someone has stated that, "Self-confidence has always been the first secret of success." Psychiatrist, Dr. Alexander Thomas, in an article "Self-Confidence—Who Needs it?" says, "Lack of self-confidence is a nationwide problem. It is perhaps the most common psychological problem in America today." Self-confidence—herein lies the wonder of the raising of the threshold of commitment. When you practice the steps of commitment and raise the threshold of commitment, you automatically gain self-confidence.

You begin by making a small but challenging commitment. You complete that commitment and see that you can be successful, then you make larger commitments and on and on. Each time you are successful you prove to yourself that you can succeed, and you gain tremendous self-confidence. The higher the threshold of commitment goes, the higher goes your self-esteem and the more productive you become. Wow, ain't it great! And you can do it. You can say with Paul, "I can do all things through Him who strengthens me."

11
Practical Examples

*Brethren, join in
following my example.*
Philippians 3:17

Allow me to share with you several of my personal experiences in raising my own threshold of commitment. These practical examples may help you to grow and be more successful in your adventure of possibility living.

I suppose my life has always been a "test bed" in search of the process of commitment. I have been successful in most of my ventures but not until after numerous struggles. I have suffered defeats and setbacks that would never have happened if I had known the steps of commitment and had been able to raise my threshold of commitment to a higher level. It seems that so much effort was wasted groping in the dark before I finally claimed the victories.

I became a Christian when I was 14 years old, during a small country church revival. I faltered and failed as a Christian for years. After a very poor high school education and almost flunking out of college my freshman year, I went from the dean's bad guy list to his good guy roster academically and got my degree on schedule. At the same time I received a commission in the United States Air Force as a second lieutenant. I was finally accepted for pilot training after flunking the flight physical on two counts, both eyes and ears. I was allowed to take the physical again and, after much effort to correct my hearing and sight, I passed. Following many trials, difficulties, and several near washouts, I received my wings and was a combat-ready jet fighter pilot for two years. After almost four years in the air force, with no biblical background, a degree in agriculture, and some experience as a "jet jockey," I entered a theological seminary. This was a tremendous change and required a lot of adjustment, but I finally graduated with a Master of Divinity degree.

One challenging experience in commitment came when I started from scratch a new mission church in the gambling capital of the world, Las Vegas, Nevada. However, I learned my real lessons in commitment as a chaplain, husband, and father during the years of active duty in the air force. I wrestled with commitments as I went through seven permanent changes of station, one of which was 15 months of total separation from my family, and through a host of difficult but rewarding ministry situations. I was making progress in my commitments, but it was still a trial and error affair.

Through the years I had always considered myself a very successful individual. However, after attending the Robert H. Schuller Institute for Successful Church Leadership in August 1976, I found myself weighed in the balance and found wanting. At the institute, I was exposed firsthand to possibility thinking in action. I rapidly learned that I was not living up to my possibilities. Though it was a real shock to me, I realized I had not developed even a fraction of my potential.

When I was stationed at Williams Air Force Base in Arizona, I used to attend the monthly ministerial meetings in the local community. Often one of my pastor friends would ask me how things were going at the base chapel. Once I jokingly answered,

"Oh, we are only running at half-throttle out there, because we don't want to steal all your church members." After exposure to possibility thinking and the searching questions at the institute, I learned I was bragging when I made that statement; I truthfully was operating at much less than half-throttle. I had hardly gotten out of first gear.

After the institute at Garden Grove Community Church, I started reading, studying, and searching. It was then that I developed the concept of the threshold of commitment and the steps of commitment. I conscientiously started practicing and testing what I had learned about commitment. Immediately I found I was able to accomplish things that earlier I had felt were impossible for me. I found myself fulfilling dreams I normally would not have even dared to dream. I broke old negative habits, I established new positive ones. I changed attitudes, I enlarged mental abilities, my health was rejuvenated, my physical vigor was multiplied, and my spiritual sensitivity and power were invigorated. In short, abundant life and possibility living began to become a reality. My threshold of commitment was on the rise.

The first major commitment I made and completed, using a worksheet, was a real personal victory for me. It gave me tremendous self-confidence and greatly deepened my spiritual life. It was a commitment to read through the Bible in a year. This particular commitment was a specific victory, because I had attempted to read through the Scripture several times in the last few years but had failed miserably each time. I had read through the entire Bible several times earlier in my Christian life and felt it was very profitable but had somehow fallen into failure this time. I felt a real need to study the Bible all the way through again and felt guilty because I had not done so. Each time I tried I violated the steps of the process of commitment and gave it up only a few weeks after I started.

This time I did it right. I followed the steps in the process to the letter. I wrote out the commitment, set targets, established a precise moment of commitment, got a dramatic start, and proceeded to make the commitment public. At the time I was conducting two Sunday morning worship services, one at 8:30 A.M and the other at 10:30 A.M. Attending the early service was a small but faithful group of conscientious Christians whom I greatly admired; so I publicly shared my commitment with them in a service. I asked for their prayers and their encouragement— and they gave it. In fact, several of them made the same commitment with me. Hardly a week passed before several of them asked me how I was doing and gave me a pep talk. Those who had made the same commitment would compare progress reports and encourage each other.

I was excited about the commitment and was enjoying it tremendously, so I almost immediately doubled my daily reading. I had a new, colorful, modern edition of the Bible, marked with a bright red bookmark with the Christian symbol of the fish on it and the words, "It's possible," on the fish. What positive inspiration it was. I kept the Bible on my desk at home and read about six or eight chapters a day, reading every morning and every night. I enjoyed it so much and got so much out of it that I looked forward to reading every night and every morning. I stayed with the commitment and enjoyed fruit along the way and ended up reading through the Bible in five months! I was so elated by the success that I immediately started reading the New Testament again. I still read a portion of Scripture every morning and every night as a result of that commitment. I would recommend it to every Christian. It gives a lot of Christian confidence to read from cover to cover and to refresh your mind with all the wonderful stories and teachings in the Word of God. It's a great adventure.

I have made several interesting discoveries from my running

commitments that have raised my own threshold of commitment and helped me understand the process. I started my running commitment on October 21, 1968, long before I outlined the process of commitment. Fortunately, I unknowingly followed all of the steps of the process fairly closely, including putting my commitment in writing and making it public. The very fact that I kept systematic records and made the commitment public made it possible for me to be successful all these years. It was my running experience, more than perhaps anything else, that helped me to formulate the actual steps and sub-steps in the process of commitment.

It was the specific commitment to run a marathon that taught me what tremendous potential each one of us has inherent within us. With a specific written commitment, high targets and goals, and assistance from others, I was able to go almost four times further than I had thought I could go after years of conditioning and experience as a runner. In fact, for several years I honestly believed my limit of endurance was three miles, and, of course, it was only as long as I believed it was. Right now, I honestly do not know what my real inherent potential is. It may be 100 miles! My suspicion is that it is as far as I can believe and am willing to commit myself to go.

There is one other rather unique lesson I have learned recently that I would like to share with you. That lesson is: even deep-seated, long-standing attitudes, feelings, and emotions can be changed by making specific commitments. While reading the September, 1978, issue of *Positive Living Magazine,* I was impressed by Joe Alexander's 12 attributes of a potent person. I felt I needed growth in all of the 12 areas, but I was especially weak in some specific areas. I took out a commitment worksheet and typed the 12 attributes and their explanation on the back. I then made a specific commitment to grow in each of these areas.

Next I graded myself on each attribute on a scale of 1 to 10. On some of them I was as low as 6 on the scale. My target was to reach a level of at least 9 by October 1980. I read them and reread them and concentrated on improving the weak attributes until I actually began to feel attitudes and feelings changing. I reviewed the commitment periodically and regraded myself on each point. Occasionally I would slip back a point on one or two attributes, but finally the attitudes, emotions, and abilities began to change and the targets were reached. I feel the changes are permanent. As a result, I am a more potent person, and my friends and family are aware of the changes every day.

I have made many more specific commitments and continue to do so. Some of the ones I have in my workbook are lifetime commitments, some will take years to complete, and others are short-term and are yielding fruit regularly. I have made commitments to eat more wholesome natural foods, to read certain books, to establish a better prayer life, to be a better father and husband, to think more positively in specific areas, and to run a given number of miles in a given year. I also made firm and specific commitments to write this book, to get it published, to start my own corporation, to become a better public speaker, and many more personal and professional accomplishments.

I know without any doubt that these concepts work for myself and others because I have witnessed them in action. For instance, there is a young husband who has made a specific commitment that (1) has saved his marriage, (2) is making his life richer, and (3) is making him a better witness for Christ. He has written the commitment out on a worksheet and has two copies of it. One is in a frame on the wall of his home to remind him of his commitment and as a public testimony. The other is beside his bed on a nightstand where he can keep his progress reports up to date. He is a new person today because of that commitment. He is growing and will continue to grow as he learns to use the process better and raise his threshold.

A young lady has discovered and is developing her solo voice to praise Christ in worship because of her discovery of possibility living. A gentleman is committed to inventing the "impossible" as a result of the question, "Why not?" Another young man has gained new self-confidence and physical vigor because of a specific commitment to aerobic exercises after years of frustration and failures. A couple is accepting responsibilities in Christian service and making a tremendous contribution as they grow in stewardship through commitment.

There are those who are reading through the Bible and studying Scripture because of specific commitments to growth. Others are permanently losing weight who didn't believe it was possible before they discovered possibility living through commitment. Some have literally changed the course of their lives, because they have realized they must commit themselves and become involved if they are going to grow and develop their potential.

Commitment is not corny at all. It is converting and life-changing. It will make you "great" if you will put it into practical use in your personal life. All those whose lives have been enriched through commitment join the apostle Paul in saying, "Brethren, join in following my example" (Phil. 3:17).

12
Your Threshold of Commitment Workbook

Let all things be done properly and in an orderly manner.
1 Corinthians 14:40

The pages that follow are your personal workbook. The bibliography and worksheets are included to help you get started in raising your threshold of commitment. If you genuinely want to be more productive and successful in life—if you are serious about possibility living through commitment—then use the worksheets systematically to give you direction and momentum. Don't be bashful or afraid to write out your commitments and what you want in life. Written goals are one of the secrets of the super successful.

Your success is strictly up to you. No one else is going to live for you. No one else is going to be successful for you. You have to do it yourself. It is almost trite to say that you can be successful, because you know you can. All you have to do is learn to think big and commit yourself to your God-given ideas. Commitment is the master key to success, and you are now the holder of the master key. So use it in conjunction with your knowledge, enthusiasm, motivation, possibility thinking, and desire to live life to its fullest. Open those double-locked doors and you will find abundant life.

Congratulations, I knew you could do it!

Bibliography

Books

Allen, James. *As a Man Thinketh*. Kansas City: Hallmark Cards, Inc., 1968.

Brothers, Joyce. *How to Get Whatever You Want Out of Life*. New York: Random House, Inc., 1978.

Cooper, Kenneth H. *Aerobics*. New York: Bantam Books, 1968.

————*The Aerobic Way*. New York: Bantam Books, 1977.

Hill, Napoleon. *Think and Grow Rich*. New York: Fawcett Books, 1960.

Peale, Norman Vincent. *The Power of Positive Thinking*. Old Tappan, NJ: Fleming H. Revell Company, 1952.

Peale, Norman Vincent. *The Positive Power of Jesus Christ*. New York: Guidepost, 1980.

Schuller, Robert H. *Move Ahead with Possibility Thinking*. New York: Doubleday Company, Inc., 1967.

————*You Can Become the Person You Want to Be*. New York: Hawthorn Books, Inc., 1973.

————*The Greatest Possibility Thinker That Ever Lived.* Old Tappan, NJ: Fleming H. Revell Company, 1973.

————*Reach Out for New Life.* New York: Hawthorn Books, Inc., 1977.

Trueblood, Elton. *The Company of the Committed.* New York: Harper and Row Publishers, 1961.

Ziglar, Zig. *See You At the Top.* Gretna, LA: Pelican Publishing Company, 1975.

Cassette Tapes

Conklin, Bob. *The Positive Mind!* Minneapolis: Personal Dynamics Institute, 1975.

Nightingale, Earl. *Lead the Field.* Chicago: Nightingale-Conant Corporation, 1972.

————*The Strangest Secret* and *The Mind of Man.* Chicago: Nightingale-Conant Corporation, 1972.

Waitley, Denis. *The Psychology of Winning.* Chicago: Nightingale-Conant Corporation, 1979.

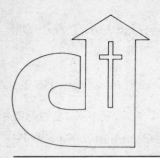

Steps of Commitment

1. *CHOOSE* YOUR COMMITMENT WISELY
   A. Be certain you have the facts.
   B. Imagine possibilities if you do or do not commit yourself.
   C. Ask, Will this be a great thing for myself, others, and God's kingdom?
   D. Ask, What are the moral, ethical, and spiritual obligations?
   E. Seek guidance through Scripture and prayer.
2. *COMMIT* YOURSELF FIRMLY AND SPECIFICALLY
   A. Do not overcommit yourself.
   B. Target the fulfillment of your commitment.
   C. Establish a precise moment of commitment.
   D. Get a definite start.
   E. Let yourself get excited about your commitment.
3. *COORDINATE* ALL YOUR RESOURCES TOWARD YOUR TARGETS
   A. Discover and develop your own resources.
   B. Ask for and utilize help from others.
   C. Seek and accept God's help.
4. *COMPLETE* YOUR COMMITMENT
   A. Give the commitment enough time to bear fruit.
   B. Stop the commitment only when completed or destructive.
   C. Quit a commitment only with a rationale decision.
   D. Enjoy your commitment.

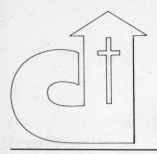

Steps of Commitment Worksheet

1. *CHOOSE* YOUR COMMITMENT WISELY
2. *COMMIT* YOURSELF FIRMLY AND SPECIFICALLY
3. *COORDINATE* ALL YOUR RESOURCES TOWARD YOUR TARGETS
4. *COMPLETE* YOUR COMMITMENT

My commitment is _____

My targets are _____
_____
_____

My precise moment of commitment is _____

    Signature _____

My definite start was _____
_____
_____

Progress reports: _____
_____
_____
_____
_____
_____
_____
_____

☐ Commitment completed _____
                                       Date

Steps of Commitment
Worksheet

1. *CHOOSE* YOUR COMMITMENT WISELY
2. *COMMIT* YOURSELF FIRMLY AND SPECIFICALLY
3. *COORDINATE* ALL YOUR RESOURCES TOWARD YOUR TARGETS
4. *COMPLETE* YOUR COMMITMENT

My commitment is _____

My targets are _____
_____
_____

My precise moment of commitment is _____

    Signature _____

My definite start was _____
_____
_____

Progress reports: _____
_____
_____
_____
_____
_____
_____
_____

☐ Commitment completed _____
Date

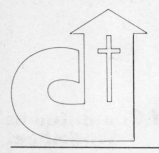

Steps of Commitment
Worksheet

1. *CHOOSE* YOUR COMMITMENT WISELY
2. *COMMIT* YOURSELF FIRMLY AND SPECIFICALLY
3. *COORDINATE* ALL YOUR RESOURCES TOWARD YOUR TARGETS
4. *COMPLETE* YOUR COMMITMENT

My commitment is _____

My targets are _____
_____
_____

My precise moment of commitment is _____

    Signature _____

My definite start was _____
_____
_____

Progress reports: _____
_____
_____
_____
_____
_____
_____
_____

☐ Commitment completed _____
                          Date

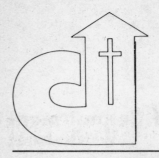

Steps of Commitment
Worksheet

1. *CHOOSE* YOUR COMMITMENT WISELY
2. *COMMIT* YOURSELF FIRMLY AND SPECIFICALLY
3. *COORDINATE* ALL YOUR RESOURCES TOWARD YOUR TARGETS
4. *COMPLETE* YOUR COMMITMENT

My commitment is _____

My targets are _____

_____

_____

My precise moment of commitment is _____

    Signature _____

My definite start was _____

_____

_____

Progress reports: _____

_____

_____

_____

_____

_____

_____

_____

☐ Commitment completed _____
                                     Date

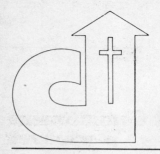

Steps of Commitment Worksheet

1. *CHOOSE* YOUR COMMITMENT WISELY
2. *COMMIT* YOURSELF FIRMLY AND SPECIFICALLY
3. *COORDINATE* ALL YOUR RESOURCES TOWARD YOUR TARGETS
4. *COMPLETE* YOUR COMMITMENT

My commitment is _____

My targets are _____

_____

_____

My precise moment of commitment is _____

 Signature _____

My definite start was _____

_____

_____

Progress reports: _____

_____

_____

_____

_____

_____

_____

_____

☐ Commitment completed _____
                              Date

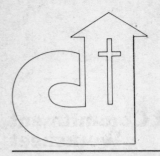

Steps of Commitment
Worksheet

1. *CHOOSE* YOUR COMMITMENT WISELY
2. *COMMIT* YOURSELF FIRMLY AND SPECIFICALLY
3. *COORDINATE* ALL YOUR RESOURCES TOWARD YOUR TARGETS
4. *COMPLETE* YOUR COMMITMENT

My commitment is _____

My targets are _____
_____
_____

My precise moment of commitment is _____

    Signature _____

My definite start was _____
_____
_____

Progress reports: _____
_____
_____
_____
_____
_____
_____
_____

☐ Commitment completed _____
                       Date

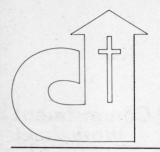

Steps of Commitment
Worksheet

1. *CHOOSE* YOUR COMMITMENT WISELY
2. *COMMIT* YOURSELF FIRMLY AND SPECIFICALLY
3. *COORDINATE* ALL YOUR RESOURCES TOWARD YOUR TARGETS
4. *COMPLETE* YOUR COMMITMENT

My commitment is _____

My targets are _____
_____
_____

My precise moment of commitment is _____

    Signature _____

My definite start was _____
_____
_____

Progress reports: _____
_____
_____
_____
_____
_____
_____

☐ Commitment completed _____
Date

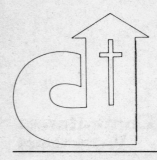

Steps of Commitment Worksheet

1. *CHOOSE* YOUR COMMITMENT WISELY
2. *COMMIT* YOURSELF FIRMLY AND SPECIFICALLY
3. *COORDINATE* ALL YOUR RESOURCES TOWARD YOUR TARGETS
4. *COMPLETE* YOUR COMMITMENT

My commitment is _____

My targets are _____

_____

_____

My precise moment of commitment is _____

    Signature _____

My definite start was _____

_____

_____

Progress reports: _____

_____

_____

_____

_____

_____

_____

_____

☐ Commitment completed _____

                                                  Date

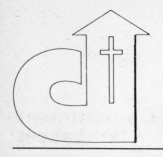

Steps of Commitment Worksheet

1. *CHOOSE* YOUR COMMITMENT WISELY
2. *COMMIT* YOURSELF FIRMLY AND SPECIFICALLY
3. *COORDINATE* ALL YOUR RESOURCES TOWARD YOUR TARGETS
4. *COMPLETE* YOUR COMMITMENT

My commitment is _____

My targets are _____

_____

_____

My precise moment of commitment is _____

   Signature _____

My definite start was _____

_____

_____

Progress reports: _____

_____

_____

_____

_____

_____

_____

_____

☐ Commitment completed _____

Date

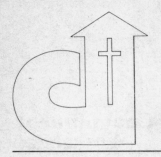

Steps of Commitment
Worksheet

1. *CHOOSE* YOUR COMMITMENT WISELY
2. *COMMIT* YOURSELF FIRMLY AND SPECIFICALLY
3. *COORDINATE* ALL YOUR RESOURCES TOWARD YOUR TARGETS
4. *COMPLETE* YOUR COMMITMENT

My commitment is _____

My targets are _____
_____
_____

My precise moment of commitment is _____

    Signature _____

My definite start was _____
_____
_____

Progress reports: _____
_____
_____
_____
_____
_____
_____
_____

☐ Commitment completed _____
                              Date